MW00588032

"This excellent introduction to interpreting the Bible provides me with an answer to the question I am so often asked: 'Can you help me understand the Bible? I don't know how to read it or make sense of it.' Plummer's short but substantive explanation of the basic principles for biblical interpretation will prove to be an immensely practical resource for the body of Christ. Highly recommended!"

—Sam Storms, Senior Pastor,
Bridgeway Church,
Oklahoma City, OK

"Plummer is a clear and evenhanded guide to foundational and complex interpretational issues."

—Andy Naselli,
Research Manager for D. A. Carson,
Administrator of *Themelios*

"These booklets from Rob Plummer are a gift to the church of Jesus Christ. Few can take the fruits of faithful scholarship and serve them in an eminently accessible form for the benefit of the church. Rob Plummer succeeds admirably at this very point. These booklets have my highest recommendation."

—Jason C. Meyer, Pastor for Preaching & Vision,
Bethlehem Baptist Church,
Minneapolis, MN

UNDERSTANDING *the* BIBLE

A Guide to Reading and Enjoying Scripture

ROBERT L. PLUMMER

Kregel
Publications

Understanding the Bible: A Guide to Reading and Enjoying Scripture
© 2013 by Robert L. Plummer

Published by Kregel Publications, a division of Kregel, Inc., P.O. Box 2607, Grand Rapids, MI 49501.

All rights reserved. No part of this book may be reproduced, stored in a retrieval system, or transmitted in any form or by any means—electronic, mechanical, photo-copy, recording, or otherwise—without written permission of the publisher, except for brief quotations in printed reviews.

This book contains material adapted from *40 Questions About Interpreting the Bible*, © 2010 by Robert L. Plummer.

All Scripture quotations, unless otherwise indicated, are from the *Holy Bible, New International Version*®. Copyright © 1973, 1978, 1984 by International Bible Society. Used by permission of Zondervan. All rights reserved.

Scripture quotations marked NASB are from the New American Standard Bible®. Copyright © 1960, 1962, 1963, 1968, 1971, 1972, 1973, 1975, 1977, 1995 by The Lockman Foundation. Used by permission. www.Lockman.org

Scripture quotations marked NLT are from the *Holy Bible*, New Living Translation, copyright © 1996, 2004, 2007 by Tyndale House Foundation. Used by permission of Tyndale House Publishers, Inc., Carol Stream, Illinois 60188. All rights reserved.

The Greek font SymbolU and the Hebrew font New JerusalemU are both available from www.linguistsoftware.com/lgku.htm, +1-425-775-1130.

ISBN 978-0-8254-4316-9

Printed in the United States of America

13 14 15 16 17 / 5 4 3 2 1

Contents

Introduction 7

1. The Importance of Biblical Interpretation 9

2. General Principles for Interpreting the Bible 17

3. Improving as an Interpreter of the Bible 33

4. Helpful Books and Tools for Interpreting the Bible 45

5. Determining the Meaning of a Biblical Text 57

6. The Role of the Holy Spirit in Interpreting the Bible 73

7. The Overarching Message of the Bible 83

Select Bibliography 95

Introduction

"**Y**ou're ruining my preaching, Doc!"

So exclaimed a student in the front row of my Biblical Interpretation class. This cry of consternation was actually a great compliment to me. Through my instruction, the student had come to realize that he would have to leave behind his haphazard sermonizing in favor of "correctly handling the word of truth" (2 Tim. 2:15). Indeed, if we would never distort a dear family member's words, why would we be less careful with the words of the living God recorded in Scripture?

The purpose of this short book is to explain the essential ingredients of faithful biblical interpretation. This seven-chapter study was condensed from my larger work, *40 Questions About Interpreting the Bible* (Kregel, 2010). For this new format, the material has been updated and reworked slightly. The main benefit of this condensed layout is to provide a brief, accurate, and affordable resource for individuals, churches, or small groups interested in foundational questions about the Bible.

For persons leading a study based on this book, additional free resources (PowerPoint files, answers to discussion questions, lesson plans, etc.) may be found under the "Resources" tab at www.robplummer.com.

I want to express thanks to Rod Elledge for proofreading and to my former professors, Robert Stein and Mark Seifrid, who obeyed 2 Timothy 2:2.

CHAPTER 1

The Importance of Biblical Interpretation

Appealing to the same Bible, Christians, Mormons, and Jehovah's Witnesses can reach amazingly divergent conclusions. Christians, for example, believe there is only one God, a triune Being (Father, Son, and Spirit) who has existed and will exist forever. Mormons cite verses to assert that the God of the Bible is just one among countless deities and that we ourselves, if male, can also become gods. Jehovah's Witnesses claim it is blasphemy to say that Jesus or the Spirit is a divine person. Even people who claim the name of Christian disagree vehemently as to whether the Bible condemns homosexual behavior. On another level, believing Christians can be puzzled after reading an Old Testament text regulating infectious skin diseases or land redistribution in ancient Israel. How are such texts applicable today? Clearly, it is not enough to simply say, "I believe the Bible." Proper interpretation of the Bible is essential.

What Is Interpretation?

To interpret a document is to express its meaning through speaking or writing. To engage in interpretation assumes that there is, in fact, a proper and improper meaning of a text and that care must be taken to not misrepresent the meaning. When dealing with the Scriptures, to properly interpret a text is to faithfully convey the inspired human author's meaning of the text, while not neglecting divine intent.

The Scriptures Show the Need for Biblical Interpretation

Numerous texts in the Bible clearly demonstrate that there is both a correct and incorrect way to understand the Scriptures. A sampling of these texts with brief commentary appears below.

- *2 Timothy 2:15: "Do your best to present yourself to God as one approved, a workman who does not need to be ashamed and who correctly handles the word of truth."* In this verse, Paul exhorts Timothy to "correctly handle," or "rightly interpret" (*orthotomounta*), the word of truth, that is, the Scriptures. Such a warning implies that the Scriptures might be wrongly handled or wrongly interpreted.

- *Psalm 119:18: "Open my eyes that I may see wonderful things in your law."* Here the psalmist pleads that the Lord would allow him to understand and delight in the meaning of Scripture. This appeal shows that the experience of joyful understanding of Scripture is not universal or automatic.

- *2 Peter 3:15–16: "Bear in mind that our Lord's patience means salvation, just as our dear brother Paul also wrote you with the wisdom that God gave him. He writes the same way in all his letters, speaking in them of these matters. His letters contain some things that are hard to understand, which ignorant and unstable people distort, as they do the other Scriptures, to their own destruction."* It is clear from Peter's instructions that it is possible to distort the meaning of Scripture. And, far from countenancing such interpretive license, Peter says that perverting the meaning of Scripture is a sin of serious consequence.

- *Ephesians 4:11–13: "It was [Christ] who gave some to be apostles, some to be prophets, some to be evangelists, and some to be pastors and teachers, to prepare God's people for works of service, so that the body of Christ may be built up until we all reach unity in the faith and in the knowledge of the Son of God and become mature, attaining to the whole measure of the fullness of Christ."* If the Scriptures were automatically properly understood by all, there would be no need for divinely gifted teachers to instruct and edify the church. God's provision of a teaching office in the church demonstrates the need for people who can properly understand and explain the Bible.

- *2 Timothy 4:2–3: "Preach the Word; be prepared in season and out of season; correct, rebuke and encourage—with great patience and careful instruction. For the time will come when men will not put up with sound doctrine. Instead, to suit their own desires, they will gather around them a great number of teachers to say what their itching ears want to hear."* Paul's instructions to Timothy show that there is a correct way to preach Scriptural revelation, and there will also be distorters of that revelation.

Language and Culture Show the Need for Biblical Interpretation

Most persons who received a document like this from Genesis 1:1:

בְּרֵאשִׁית בָּרָא אֱלֹהִים אֵת הַשָּׁמַיִם וְאֵת הָאָרֶץ׃

or this from Matthew 1:1:

Βίβλος γενέσεως Ἰησοῦ Χριστοῦ υἱοῦ Δαυὶδ υἱοῦ Ἀβραάμ

would immediately recognize their need for a translation of the text. In some ways, translation is the most fundamental form of interpretation. The text in its original language is unintelligible to a new audience, so it must be put into a new language. Yet, the translation of a text is not like the repetition of mathematical rules simply with different symbols. All languages have cultural elements and assumed historical backgrounds that cannot be expressed with the same number of words or exactly parallel grammatical constructions. Thus there is the need for additional study, explanation, and interpretation of a text. For example, in Matthew 1:18, Mary and Joseph are described as engaged, yet in Matthew 1:19, Joseph ponders divorcing Mary. Unlike modern American engagement customs, ancient Jewish customs necessitated a divorce to break a betrothal. Certainly, this concept can be explained, but it is difficult to convey succinctly in a translation. Indeed, even when communicating in one's native language, there is often need for additional clarification of ambiguous concepts.

A number of years ago, I read a report of a strange practice developing among some young Christians in China. These new believers felt that it was a sign of true faith to carry with them a small wooden cross. Apparently, on the basis of Jesus' instructions in Luke 9:23 ("If anyone would come after me, he must deny himself and take up his cross daily and follow me"), these Christians had come to think that putting a wooden cross in one's pocket was commanded by Christ. To "take up one's cross," however, is a figure of speech, meaning to deny one's own ambitions and desires in submission to the lordship of Christ.

If we are familiar with the different time periods, genres, and anticipations/fulfillments of Scripture, we are better able to confidently approach any individual part of the Bible. Assuming the unified nature of the Bible, as well as the progressive unfolding of God's plans (Heb. 1:1–3), it is clear that a person with an established understanding of God's overarching purposes will be better equipped to understand individual pieces of the story. Of course, time and study are required to attain such greater familiarity with the text.

It is sometimes said that Scripture is the best interpreter of Scripture. This means that the broader biblical context will help one properly understand any individual passage. Without knowing the entire book of 1 John, for example, 1 John 5:6 seems hopelessly obscure ("This is the one who came by water and blood—Jesus Christ. He did not come by water only, but by water and blood. And it is the Spirit who testifies, because the Spirit is the truth"). Knowing the broader context of the letter, assuming a unified message in the New Testament, and having some exposure to the cultural background of incipient Gnosticism, we can reasonably conclude that the verse affirms the divine-human nature of Christ, seen both in his baptism (water) and death/resurrection (blood).[1]

A proper understanding of the author's original meaning is also fundamental for proper application of the text today. For example, Proverbs 22:28 says, "Do not move an ancient boundary stone set up by your forefathers." As boundary stones were used to mark ancient property lines, this proverb forbids the dishonest acquisition of a neighbor's land. Applied more broadly, the text points to divine displeasure at any sneaky stealing—whether moving ancient stones, engaging in e-mail phishing schemes, or any other surreptitious theft.

---

1. See John R. W. Stott, *The Letters of John*, rev. ed., Tyndale New Testament Commentaries 19 (Grand Rapids: Eerdmans; Leicester: Inter-Varsity Press, 1988), 179–82.

The principle ("don't steal in a sneaky way") must be distilled from a culturally conditioned command ("do not move an ancient boundary stone").

Careful interpretation is important because assumed theological presuppositions often can drive interpretations. Through careful biblical interpretation, the student of Scripture can become aware of others' biases, as well as begin to acknowledge and assess his or her own hermeneutical predilections.

REFLECTION QUESTIONS

1. When reading the Bible, are you conscious of the danger of mis-interpreting it—that is, of misunderstanding it and distorting its meaning in explaining it to others?

2. How is interpreting the Bible different from interpreting any other piece of literature?

3. Consider other Christians whose interpretations of the Bible you have either read or heard. Whom do you consider the most reliable? Why?

4. What would make you a more faithful biblical interpreter?

5. Are you aware of any theological or interpretive biases you have in approaching the Scriptures? Can you defend having such biases from the Bible itself?

FOR FURTHER STUDY

Brown, Jeannine K. *Scripture as Communication: Introducing Biblical Hermeneutics.* Grand Rapids: Baker, 2007.

Fee, Gordon D., and Douglas Stuart. *How to Read the Bible for All Its Worth.* 3rd ed. Grand Rapids: Zondervan, 2003.

Köstenberger, Andreas J., and Richard D. Patterson, *Biblical Interpretation: Exploring the Hermeneutical Triad of History, Literature, and Theology.* Grand Rapids: Kregel, 2011.

Stein, Robert H. *A Basic Guide to Interpreting the Bible: Playing by the Rules.* 2nd ed. Grand Rapids: Baker, 2011.

CHAPTER 2

General Principles for Interpreting the Bible

While good biblical interpretation is better caught (that is, learned from reading and hearing those who do it well) than taught, it can be helpful to enumerate some overarching interpretive principles. Applied over time, these principles will become more second nature in your interpretation of Scripture. We will begin with more devotional aspects of Bible study (prayer, meditation, obedience) and then move to more technical or literary guidelines.

Approach the Bible in Prayer

The Scriptures tell us that the human heart is desperately wicked and deceitful (Jer. 17:9). Indeed, the basic human response to God's natural revelation (through conscience or nature) is to suppress it in idolatry (Rom. 1:18–23). Even God's people, though given a new nature and the Holy Spirit as a guide, must beware of the deceitful inclinations of their remaining sinful nature. In Psalm 119, the author, traditionally assumed to be King David, serves as a good example of honest self-assessment in his approach to the Scripture. Repeatedly, he prays for insight and redirection. Below is a list of sample petitions within the psalm. Slowly praying through selected verses in Psalm 119 is an excellent way to begin a Bible study session.

- *Verse 5:* [addressing the Lord] "Oh, that my ways were steadfast in obeying your decrees!"

- *Verse 10:* "I seek you [LORD] with all my heart; do not let me stray from your commands."

- *Verse 12:* "Praise be to you, O LORD; teach me your decrees."

- *Verses 17–20:* "Do good to your servant, and I will live; I will obey your word. Open my eyes that I may see wonderful things in your law. I am a stranger on earth; do not hide your commands from me. My soul is consumed with longing for your laws at all times."

- *Verses 34–37:* "Give me understanding, and I will keep your law and obey it with all my heart. Direct me in the path of your commands, for there I find delight. Turn my heart toward your statutes and not toward selfish gain. Turn my eyes away from worthless things; preserve my life according to your word."

The great reformer Martin Luther recognized Psalm 119 as helpful instruction for studying the Bible. He noted:

> Thus you see how David keeps praying in the above-mentioned Psalm, "Teach me, Lord, instruct me, lead me, show me," and many more words like these. Although he well knew and daily heard and read the text of Moses and other books besides, still he wants to lay hold of the real teacher of the Scriptures himself, so that he may not seize upon them pell-mell with his reason and become his own teacher. For such practice gives rise to factious spirits who allow themselves to nurture the delusion that the Scriptures are subject to them and can be easily grasped with their reason, as if they were *Markolf* or Aesop's Fables, for which no Holy Spirit and no prayers are needed.[1]

As we approach the Bible, we need to realize that sin affects all of our being—our emotions, wills, and rational faculties. We can easily deceive ourselves or be deceived by others. We need the Holy Spirit to instruct and guide us. Thus, prayer is the essential starting point for any study of the Bible.[2]

---

1. Martin Luther, "Preface to the Wittenberg Edition of Luther's German Writings" (1539), in *Martin Luther's Basic Theological Writings*, ed. Timothy F. Lull and William R. Russell, 3rd ed. (Minneapolis: Fortress, 2012), 41.
2. Spurgeon advised young pastors, "Praying is the best studying. Luther said so of old—'*Bene orasse est bene studuisse*,' and the well-worn proverb will bear repeating. Pray over Scripture; it is as the treading of grapes in the wine-vat, the

Read the Bible as a Book That Points to Jesus

In a debate with the Jewish religious leaders in Jerusalem, Jesus said, "You diligently study the Scriptures because you think that by them you possess eternal life. These are the Scriptures that testify about me, yet you refuse to come to me to have life" (John 5:39–40; cf. Luke 24:25–27). If we study or teach any part of the Bible without reference to Jesus the Savior, we are not faithful interpreters. Of course, not every text points to Jesus in the same way. The Old Testament promises, anticipates, and prepares. Jesus noted this forward-looking dimension to all of God's prior revelation, saying, "For all the Prophets and the Law prophesied until John [the Baptist]" (Matt. 11:13). The New Testament announces the fulfillment in Christ of all of Israel's law, history, prophecies, and institutions. Every passage of Scripture must be read as a chapter in a completed book. As we know how the story wraps up (in Christ's life, death, and resurrection), we must always be asking how prior chapters lead to that culmination. When confronted by God's ultimate standard of holiness, whether in the Old or New Testament, we are always reminded of our inherent unworthiness and are pointed to the sufficiency of Christ. Our sin is the problem. Jesus is the solution.

Let Scripture Interpret Scripture

The hermeneutical guideline of Scripture interpreting Scripture has long been espoused by Christian interpreters, going back at least to Augustine (A.D. 354–430) and Irenaeus (A.D. 130–200).[3] If we believe that all the Bible is inspired by God and thus non-contradictory, passages of Scripture that are less clear should be interpreted with reference to those that are more transparent in meaning. Cults and heretical groups often seize upon a few obscure texts, ascribe to them questionable meaning, and then interpret the remainder of the Bible through these aberrant lenses.

Another dimension of letting Scripture interpret Scripture means listening to the full panoply of texts that touch upon a subject.

---

threshing of corn on the barn floor, the melting of gold from the ore" (C. H. Spurgeon, *Lectures to My Students: Complete and Unabridged* [London: Marshall, Morgan & Scott, n.d.; reprint, Grand Rapids: Zondervan, 1954], 86).

3. Bernard Ramm, *Protestant Biblical Interpretation: A Textbook of Hermeneutics,* 3rd ed. (Grand Rapids: Baker, 1970), 36–37; and Robert M. Grant with David Tracy, *A Short History of the Interpretation of the Bible,* 2nd ed. (Philadelphia: Fortress, 1984), 49–50.

For example, if we were to read God's words to Abraham in Genesis 17:10–12, we might conclude that even today all male worshippers of God must be circumcised.[4] Yet, we read in 1 Corinthians 7:19, "Circumcision is nothing and uncircumcision is nothing. Keeping God's commands is what counts." By understanding the trajectory of Scripture (promise → fulfillment in Christ), we see that circumcision served a preparatory role for the Jewish nation but is no longer required of God's people. As the author of Hebrews says, "The law is only a shadow of the good things that are coming—not the realities themselves" (Heb. 10:1). Paul can circumcise a coworker as a means of strategic missionary accommodation to unregenerate Jews (Acts 16:3), but when the basis of salvation is at stake, Paul is unbending (Gal. 2:3). This brief survey demonstrates how a nuanced understanding of a subject requires the consideration of multiple biblical texts that touch upon it.

Meditate on the Bible

The Bible is not a book for superficial reading. While it is certainly beneficial to read large portions of Scripture in one sitting, no biblical diet is complete without extended rumination on a smaller portion of text. Scripture itself is filled with instructions on such a meditative approach. Drawing from Psalm 119, Martin Luther noted this pattern.

> Second, [in your study of the Bible,] you should meditate, that is, not only in your heart, but also externally, by actually repeating and comparing oral speech and literal words of the book, reading and rereading them with diligent attention and reflection, so that you may see what the Holy Spirit means by them. And take care that you do not grow weary or think that you have done enough when you have read, heard, and spoken them once or twice, and that you have complete understanding. You will never be a particularly good theologian if you do that, for you will be like untimely fruit which falls to the ground before it is half ripe.

---

4. Genesis 17:10–12, "This is my covenant with you and your descendants after you, the covenant you are to keep: Every male among you shall be circumcised. You are to undergo circumcision, and it will be the sign of the covenant between me and you. For the generations to come every male among you who is eight days old must be circumcised."

Thus you see in this same Psalm [119] how David constantly boasts that he will talk, meditate, speak, sing, hear, read, by day and night and always, about nothing except God's Word and commandments. For God will not give you his Spirit without the external Word; so take your cue from that. His command to write, preach, read, hear, sing, speak, etc., outwardly was not given in vain.[5]

It is instructive that many Christians have found it best to start their prayers with quiet and sustained reflection on a small portion of Scripture. We are reminded that we come to God with empty hands. God himself provides the words for our prayers in the Bible. The Puritan Thomas Manton (1620–1677) wrote,

Meditation is a middle sort of duty between the word and prayer, and hath respect to both. The word feedeth meditation, and meditation feedeth prayer; we must hear that we be not erroneous, and meditate that we be not barren. These duties must always go hand in hand; meditation must follow hearing and precede prayer. To hear and not to meditate is unfruitful. We may hear and hear, but it is like putting a thing into a bag with holes. . . . It is rashness to pray and not to meditate. What we take in by the word we digest by meditation and let out by prayer. These three duties must be so ordered that one may not jostle out the other. Men are barren, dry, and sapless in their prayer for want of exercising themselves in holy thoughts.[6]

Approach the Bible in Faith and Obedience

The Bible is not a philosophy textbook to be debated; it is a revelation from God to be believed and obeyed. As we believe and obey God's Word, we will experience not only joy but also, more importantly, God's blessing, or approval. James writes,

Do not merely listen to the word, and so deceive yourselves. Do what it says. Anyone who listens to the word but does not do what it says is like a man who looks at his face in a mirror and, after looking at himself, goes away and immediately forgets what he looks like. But

---

5. Luther, "Preface," 41.
6. Thomas Manton, *The Complete Works of Thomas Manton*, vol. 17, *Sermons on Several Texts of Scripture* (reprint, Birmingham, AL: Solid Ground Christian Books, 2008), 272–73.

the man who looks intently into the perfect law that gives freedom, and continues to do this, not forgetting what he has heard, but doing it—he will be blessed in what he does. (James 1:22–25)

At the same time, we must remember that obedience to God's Word can never be brought about by increased human effort. Regeneration and divine empowerment are necessary to believe and obey God's Word. Obedience is possible only through Christ. As the apostle John writes, "This is love for God: to obey his commands. And his commands are not burdensome, for everyone born of God overcomes the world. This is the victory that has overcome the world, even our faith. Who is it that overcomes the world? Only he who believes that Jesus is the Son of God" (1 John 5:3–5).

The person who reads Scripture and does not obey it is self-deceived (James 1:22). To claim to know God while consistently and consciously disobeying his Word is to demonstrate the falseness of one's claim. The apostle John writes, "The man who says, 'I know him,' but does not do what he commands is a liar, and the truth is not in him" (1 John 2:4).

Responding with faith and obedience, specifically through difficulties, seems to be one of God's chosen means of maturing his people (Rom. 5:1–11; James 1:1–12; 1 Peter 1:1–12). As we encounter trials in life and meet those difficulties trusting in God and his Word, we can expect the Lord to conform us more into the image of his Son. We can be comforted by the words of Paul in Romans 8:28–29: "And we know that in all things God works for the good of those who love him, who have been called according to his purpose. For those God foreknew he also predestined to be conformed to the likeness of his Son, that he might be the firstborn among many brothers."

Martin Luther noted that the many references to David's trials and enemies in Psalm 119 are instructive for the Christian facing similar situations. He wrote:

Thus you see how David, in the Psalm mentioned, complains so often about all kinds of enemies, arrogant princes or tyrants, false spirits and factions, whom he must tolerate because he meditates, that is, because he is occupied with God's Word (as has been said) in all manner of ways. For as soon as God's Word takes root and grows in you, the devil will harry you, and will make a real doctor of you, and by his assaults will teach you to seek and love God's

Word. I myself (if you will permit me, mere mouse-dirt to be min-gled with pepper) am deeply indebted to my papists that through the devil's raging they have beaten, oppressed, and distressed me so much. That is to say, they have made a fairly good theologian of me, which I would not have become otherwise. And I heartily grant them what they have won in return for making this of me, honor, victory, and triumph, for that's the way they wanted it.[7]

Like Luther, we can meet the troubles of life with trust in God and a reliance on him to obey his Word.

Take Note of the Biblical Genre You Are Reading

If your son were to come home from school and claim to have a ton of homework, you would not discipline him for lying. You would understand that he is using hyperbole to express his strong emo-tions. In the same way, we need to approach the Bible as sympathetic readers, respecting the various genres and authorial assumptions that accompany such genres. For example, the genre of proverbs generally assumes exceptions. Proverbs are wise advice, not fail-proof prom-ises. For example, we read in Proverbs 10:4, "Lazy hands make a man poor, but diligent hands bring wealth." All of us can think of examples from our lives that confirm this proverb. At the same time, most of us likely know a few lazy, rich people. Such exceptions do not make the proverb false. Rather, such exceptions confirm the general rule. Proverbs 10:4 is not a promissory note. Proverbs offer wise advice for ordering our lives, but most of them assume exceptions.

The genre of historical narrative also includes a number of au-thorial assumptions. For example, the biblical authors employ histor-ical narrative to report many events of which they do not necessarily approve. The author of Judges clearly does not think sacrificing one's daughter is a good thing (Judg. 11), though he fails to comment on Jephthah's actions in the immediate context. The repeated cycle of disobedience in Judges, along with the summary statement ("In those days Israel had no king; everyone did as he saw fit" [Judg. 21:25]), cue the reader that both God and the author are not pleased with Jephthah's actions. Similarly, many Scriptures teach that drunken-ness is wrong, though the apostle John does not feel the need to note its impropriety in John 2:10, where there is a passing reference to

7. Luther, "Preface," 41–42.

inebriation. (A friend once appealed to John 2:10 to make a "biblical" case for excessive drinking!) The author of a historical narrative does not always give explicit sanction or condemnation for behavior reported. A careful reading of the whole work is often necessary to understand the purpose of smaller portions. One must thoughtfully determine what is simply reported and what is intended as normative.

The study and application of interpretive guidelines for various genres is sometimes called the field of special hermeneutics. See the latter half of my more extensive text, *40 Questions About Interpreting the Bible*, for guidelines in practicing special hermeneutics.

Be Aware of Historical or Cultural Background Issues

The sixty-six books of the Bible often assume a reader's familiarity with various cultural practices, geographic markers, or political figures. Thus, when an untrained reader opens up the book of Isaiah and starts reading about nations that no longer exist and obscure political alliances, he or she might close the Bible and say, "This is too hard to understand." As with any historical document, the reader of the Bible will need study aids to delve into the nuances of background issues. Of course, some of the books of the Bible assume little knowledge on the part of the reader and are quite accessible. The gospel of John, for example, is often distributed as a stand-alone evangelistic tract for this reason. Depending on one's familiarity with the Scripture, some background issues may be more or less transparent. Do you know what Passover is? Then you shouldn't have trouble with John the Baptist's description of Jesus as the (Passover) lamb (John 1:29). Are you familiar with Israel's forty years of wandering in the wilderness? Then Jesus' forty-day stay in the wilderness, where he was tested but did not sin, takes on added significance (Matt. 4:2; Luke 4:2).

As you study the Bible more, you will have less need to consult commentaries or study aids for the answers to basic questions. There are many introductory surveys of the Old and New Testaments, as well as books specifically on backgrounds, which provide a wealth of information to the curious student. See chapter 4 ("Helpful Books and Tools for Interpreting the Bible") for additional discussion on how to use outside books in studying the Bible.

In discussing Bible backgrounds, we also must note two important caveats. First, one can become so enamored with outside historical, cultural, political, or archaeological matters that he essentially ends up using the Bible as a springboard for extrabiblical trivia. The study of ancient Near Eastern culture, while fascinating in its own right, is not the purpose of Bible study. Not a few resources billed as helps for understanding the background of the Bible are little more than collations of interesting facts and speculations about tangentially related background issues. One must always ask: Did the biblical author really assume that his readers would know this fact? And, if he assumed his readers would know this fact, was it important for the meaning that he was trying to convey? If the answer to both of these questions is yes, then the background issue is indeed worthy of consideration.

Recently, a former student called to ask about Mark 3:13–19, where Jesus calls his twelve apostles. The student said, "I read that all Jewish boys were trained to be rabbis, and if they performed well enough, then they became disciples of rabbis and eventually rabbis themselves. So, in this passage, Jesus' disciples should be understood as those who had been rejected by conventional rabbinic training. I plan to preach this passage as emphasizing that Jesus chooses persons who have failed. Am I on track?" I responded, "There are passages of Scripture that speak of God choosing the lowly and rejected in this world (1 Cor. 1:26–27), but I do not think that the inspired author, Mark, is emphasizing that point here. In what book did you read this explanation of the background of Mark 3? (Student answers . . .) Have you read a similar explanation in any other reference work or commentary? (Student answers, "No.") That alone should cause you to pause and question whether there is a basis for interpreting this text in light of background information that is not found in any text in the Bible. It appears the source from which you have gathered this information has, at the very least, oversimplified and distorted its description of first-century rabbinic training. Second, and more importantly, Mark does not in any way cue his readers that he intends us to understand this passage as teaching that Jesus chose persons rejected by other rabbis. Does the passage speak of Jesus' effective call, his demand for radical discipleship, and his delegated authority? Yes! Then preach and teach the meaning of the text—not a fanciful, distorted reconstruction of a background issue."[8] Unfortunately, in attempts to provide something fresh to their congregations, too many pastors are readily taken in by far-fetched interpretations. A pastor's time would be better spent meditating prayerfully on the text to discover genuine text-driven applications.

---

8. This report of our conversation represents the tenor and main points, not the verbatim words.

A second error one must avoid in background issues is to neglect them. In order to understand and apply a text faithfully, one often must have some awareness of the author's historical or cultural assumptions. One cannot understand the denunciations in the Minor Prophets, for example, without knowing something of Israel's history and relations to surrounding nations. And, while much of this historical background can be garnered directly from other biblical documents, an uninitiated reader will need the help of a more mature reader's summaries. A study Bible, such as *The Zondervan NIV Study Bible* or *ESV Study Bible,* provides brief but helpful comments on relevant background issues.

Pay Attention to Context

Any portion of Scripture must be read within the context of the sentence, paragraph, larger discourse unit, and entire book. The farther one moves away from the words in question, the less informative is the adduced material. Attempting to understand or apply a particular biblical phrase or verse without reference to the literary context is virtually guaranteed to result in distortion. Unfortunately, in popular Christian literature and preaching, there are many examples of such failure to respect the context of a passage. One of the most painful exhibits of such hermeneutical failure is a preacher who bullies and blusters about the authority and inerrancy of Scripture while practically denying its authority through his sloppy preaching.

If one is asked to deliver a message on 1 Corinthians 11:1 ("Follow my example, as I follow the example of Christ."), he should not simply meditate on the verse in question but begin by setting the verse in the context of Paul's argument in 1 Corinthians. Paul has been speaking of his voluntary self-denial as an apostle (1 Cor. 9:1–12) as an example for the Corinthians, whom he is calling to deny themselves of permissible food that might cause a Christian brother or sister to sin (1 Cor. 8:9–13). Paul's concern for the spread of the gospel compels him to find every way to avoid placing an obstacle in its way. No one can charge him with being motivated by greed, for he preaches without pay (1 Cor. 9:12–18). Similarly, the Corinthian Christians' concern for the spiritual well-being of others means they should be willing to forego permissible things for the spiritual benefit of others. Indeed, Christ is the supreme example of one who set aside his rights and privileges for the salvation of others (1 Cor. 11:1; cf. Mark 10:45; Phil. 2:6–11). Once we understand Paul's original meaning in context, it is easier to faithfully apply the text to our current situation. What permissible things are we being called to forego so as not to lead our weaker Christian brothers and sisters into sin? How can we give priority to the spiritual well-being and salvation of others rather than our own rights and privileges? Where are we being called to self-denial out of love for others, as were Paul, the Corinthians, and ultimately Christ?

It often has been said, "A text without a context is a pretext," meaning that a preacher will be inclined to infuse a text with his own biases if he does not allow the context to direct him to the authorial intent. I have found this true in my life. When I am given the opportunity to select a text for a sermon, I sometimes already have an idea of what I want to say. But, as I go back to the text and study it within context, prayerfully meditating over it, the direction of my message often shifts. Holding tightly to the text calls me back to the inspired author's meaning. I tell my students to hold onto the biblical text like a rider in a rodeo holds onto a bull. And, I also warn them that the only persons in the rodeo ring not on bulls are clowns. When preaching the Bible, I want to be able to place my finger on specific words and phrases in the text to justify my exhortations. I want the congregation to be persuaded by the words of Scripture, not by my rhetorical ability. The power of a sermon or Bible lesson lies in its faithfulness to the inspired text.

Read the Bible in Community

We live in an individualistic age. Yet God created us to live and worship and grow spiritually together in community. The author of Hebrews writes, "Let us not give up meeting together, as some are in the habit of doing, but let us encourage one another—and all the more as you see the Day approaching" (Heb. 10:25). Only as we live out our faith in Christ together do we come to understand with depth and clarity what God has done in and through us (Philem. 6). Similarly, we see that God has structured the church as a body and that every member of that body does not have the same function (Rom. 12:4–5). Some are more gifted as teachers (Rom. 12:7). Others are more gifted in showing mercy or serving in some other way (Rom. 12:8). While all God's people are called to read and meditate on his Word (Ps. 119:9, 105), some are specially gifted in explaining that Word and exhorting others to believe and obey it (Eph. 4:11–13). If we neglect God's grace to us in the gifting of other believers, how impoverished we will be!

Reading the Bible with fellow believers helps us to gain insights that we would otherwise miss. Also, our brothers and sisters can guard us from straying into false interpretations and misapplications.

A few years ago I visited a nearby church where a student pastor was preaching. Honestly, his sermon was not very good. Yet this pastor had the habit of inviting trusted persons in the church to give him honest feedback on his message every week. When I visited that church several months later, the pastor's sermon was surprisingly good. Though it can be painful, when a pastor opens himself up to constructive criticism on his teaching and preaching, the fruit of his humility can be a harvest of faithful and engaging messages. Many mediocre preachers will continue to preach the same dull and errant sermons over their whole lifetimes because they are too proud to seek constructive feedback.

If a pastor does not feel that members in his church can provide him sufficient feedback, he likely underestimates the degree to which the Holy Spirit has distributed gifts within his congregation. Regardless, one can always consult the commentaries of trusted pastors and theologians as dialogue partners in seeking the meaning and application of a biblical text. When one is sufficiently grounded in essential Christian doctrine, it also can be beneficial to read persons who are outside the orthodox and evangelical fold. See chapter 4 for which commentaries to buy and how to use them.

Begin the Journey of Becoming a More Faithful Interpreter

None of us can claim to be inerrant interpreters. No matter what academic degrees or experiences one has, every person stands before the Bible as a learner. Some are farther along on the journey, but that should not intimidate those who are just beginning the trip.

One way to begin the journey toward more faithful interpretation is to start small. By choosing one particular book of the Bible and spending focused time in it over a period of several weeks or months, one will begin to see the importance and benefit of careful Bible study. Make manageable goals on reading and studying the Bible. Possibly invite a friend or friends to make the sojourn alongside you. Bible study, like athletic training, is often furthered by the camaraderie and accountability of a group.

Rome was not built in a day, and a full-orbed knowledge of the Bible is not attainable through reading one book. I am reminded of a seminary student who told me that my semester-long Greek course was much more difficult than the course he could take at an extension center over five weekends. "Yes," I replied. "That is because in my class you are actually learning the material."

Sometimes, things are worth what you pay for them. To acquire a rich knowledge of Scripture, one must be willing to spend the time and energy in study. Indeed, with the psalmist, the modern student of Scripture will come to declare, "The law from your [the LORD's] mouth is more precious to me than thousands of pieces of silver and gold" (Ps. 119:72). See the next chapter for more suggestions on how to improve as an interpreter of the Bible.

REFLECTION QUESTIONS

1. What role do prayer and meditation currently play in your study of the Bible?

2. When you read the Bible, do you, either consciously or unconsciously, take into account the genre of the book you are reading?

3. With whom are you reading and discussing the Bible? How have you benefited from studying the Bible with others? If you are not studying the Bible in community, do you know of an existing small-group Bible study that you can join?

4. Can you think of an instance where additional historical or cultural background information aided you in understanding a biblical text?

5. Have you ever changed your view on what a text of the Bible means by studying the context more carefully? "A text without a context is a pretext." Can you think of an example or illustration of this maxim?

FOR FURTHER STUDY

Carson, D. A. *New Testament Commentary Survey.* 6th ed. Grand Rapids: Baker, 2007.

Fee, Gordon D., and Douglas Stuart. *How to Read the Bible for All Its Worth.* 3rd ed. Grand Rapids: Zondervan, 2003.

Ferguson, Everett. *Backgrounds of Early Christianity.* 2nd ed. Grand Rapids: Eerdmans, 1993.

Glynn, John. *Commentary and Reference Survey: A Comprehensive Guide to Biblical and Theological Resources.* 10th ed. Grand Rapids: Kregel, 2007.

Longenecker, Bruce W. *The Lost Letters of Pergamum.* Grand Rapids: Baker, 2003.

Longman, Tremper. *Old Testament Commentary Survey.* 4th ed. Grand Rapids: Baker, 2007.

Roberts, Vaughan. *God's Big Picture: Tracing the Storyline of the Bible.* Downers Grove, IL: InterVarsity Press, 2002.

CHAPTER 3

Improving as an Interpreter of the Bible

In the previous chapter, one of the interpretive guidelines I recommended was to begin the journey of becoming a more faithful interpreter. But what specific steps can you take toward becoming a more faithful interpreter?

Read the Bible

When I was thirteen years old, my mother gave me a photocopy of a handwritten guide for reading the Bible through in a year. Thus began the most important part of my theological education—immersion in Scripture.

In order to understand the Bible, one must read it. And, in order to read the individual parts of the Bible in context, one must read the whole. Thus, it is essential for any faithful interpreter of the Bible to have read the entire Bible and to continue to read through the Bible regularly. Can you imagine a teacher of Milton who admitted to having read only portions of *Paradise Lost*? How foolish it is for a minister of the gospel to seek faithfulness in expounding God's Word while remaining ignorant of the contents of that revelation.

During my freshman year in college, I attended a Bible study run by a campus ministry. The group was discussing John 3:14, "Just as Moses lifted up the snake in the desert, so the Son of Man must be lifted up." The leader of the Bible study said this verse referred to Moses picking up the serpent (which had been his rod) by the tail at the burning bush (Exod. 4:1–4). Of course, because I had already read through the Bible several times, I knew this passage referred to the bronze serpent in Numbers 21:9. I decided not to return to the campus gathering. Unfortunately, at this point in my life, my mental knowledge of the Bible far exceeded my obedience.

For reading large sections of the Bible, I recommend a modern, dynamically equivalent translation, such as the *New Living Translation*. You can start at Genesis 1 and read three or four chapters per day. By the end of the year, you will have finished the Bible. Another option is to read portions of both the Old and New Testament every day. The famous Scottish preacher Robert Murray M'Cheyne developed a reading plan that takes one through the Old Testament once and New Testament and Psalms twice over the course of a year—reading about four chapters per day. I am currently following this reading plan, which is found in an introductory section of D. A. Carson's devotional, *For the Love of God: A Daily Companion for Discovering the Riches of God's Word*, volume 1 (Wheaton, IL: Crossway, 1998). This book has a one-page devotional for each day of the year. At the top of each page is a list of Bible chapters to read for that day, according to M'Cheyne's reading plan. Carson, a leading evangelical New Testament scholar, provides insightful reflections on one chapter from the reading plan each day. Carson also has completed a second volume, *For the Love of God*, volume 2, which follows the same format. I appreciate the way he faithfully interprets the passages while showing how the small pieces fit in the overall vista of Scripture, finding ultimate fulfillment in Christ. Our church leaders have talked about using Carson's devotional for training new elders. Over the course of a year or two, the bite-size chunks of biblical theology, slowly digested, could have quite a beneficial effect on the thoughtful reader.

Read and Listen to Faithful Preaching and Teaching

As I mentioned in chapter 2, faithful interpretation is more easily caught than taught. By reading or listening to faithful expositions of Scripture, one's heart and mind are engaged. Just as the person who regularly drinks fine coffee develops a refined taste for the beverage, a person who consumes a regular diet of faithful teaching develops a mind and heart that is able to recognize good interpretation, as well as distortions.

One of the most important questions you need to ask yourself is, "Am I hearing the Bible faithfully preached and taught at my local church?" If you are not, the second question you should ask yourself is, "Why am I a member of a church where God's Word is not being taught correctly?" If you are not experiencing the edifying and sanctifying effects of biblical teaching, you are likely withering and ineffective in your spiritual life (Col. 1:28–29; 2 Peter 1:3–8). If you are receiving a regular diet of biblical edification but only from source(s) outside your church, that is a good indication that you need to seek a new church—one where the pastors faithfully shepherd the flock, feeding them from the Word of God (Acts 20:28).

Although a local church where the Bible is faithfully taught is an absolute necessity, one can also grow spiritually from reading or listening to the sermons and Bible teaching of those outside your local church. Free audio sermons are widely available on the Web. Two Web sites I recommend are www.truthforlife.org (teaching by Alistair Begg) and www.desiringgod.org (teaching by John Piper and others). There are, of course, many other gifted, faithful preachers to whom you can listen.

One also can learn much from reading sermons, commentaries, and devotionals by faithful exegetes. Certainly, the Bible is *The* Book, but God's gifting of his servants demands that we admit the usefulness of others' books as well. The famous British preacher, Charles Spurgeon (1834–1892), wrote:

> Some, under pretense of being taught of the Spirit of God, refuse to be instructed by books or by living men. This is no honoring of the Spirit of God. It is disrespect to Him, for if He gives to some of His servants more light than to others—and it is clear He does—then they are bound to give that light to others, and to use it for the good of the church. But if the other part of the church refuse to receive that light, to what end did the Spirit of God give it? This would imply that there is a mistake somewhere in the economy of God's gifts and graces, which is managed by the Holy Spirit.[1]

One way to discover useful books or resources is to ask a trusted fellow Christian. Maybe there is someone in your church who has demonstrated a mature knowledge of the Scriptures. Why not ask that person, "What good books have you read recently? Do you have any book recommendations?" For additional advice about books that will help with your Bible study, see chapter 4 ("Helpful Books and Tools for Interpreting the Bible").

---

1. Charles Spurgeon, *Words of Counsel for Christian Workers* (Pasadena, TX: Pilgrim Publications, 1985), 112–13.

Understand the Relationship Between Faith and Understanding

The early church leader Augustine (A.D. 354–430) advised, *Crede, ut intelligas* ("Believe in order that you may understand").[2] Similarly, Anselm (ca. 1033–1109) said, "For I do not seek to understand in order to believe; I believe in order to understand. For I also believe that 'Unless I believe, I shall not understand.'"[3] God demands that we approach him in faith and receive his revelation with trust. Indeed, to reject God's revelation is nothing other than calling God a liar (1 John 1:10); it is the embracing of idolatry, the exaltation of something or someone above God (Rom. 1:18–32).

This does not mean that you cannot come to God with the honesty of your emotions and questions. The lament psalms (e.g., Pss. 13, 74, 142) are prime examples of such raw honesty before God. Indeed, roughly one-third of the psalms express lament. But even in the midst of darkness, questions, and trials, the psalmist consistently affirms, "But as for me, I trust in you" (Ps. 55:23).

The Scriptures demand that humans approach God in a humble attitude of dependence. What other posture could finite creatures take before their infinite, holy, and all-powerful Creator? The author of Hebrews warns, "And without faith it is impossible to please God, because anyone who comes to him must believe that he exists and that he rewards those who earnestly seek him" (Heb. 11:6). Like the father who brought his demon-possessed son to Jesus for healing, we may have to cry with honesty, "I do believe; help me overcome my unbelief!" (Mark 9:24).

As we seek God's assistance to understand, believe, and obey the Scriptures, a posture of humble faith is absolutely essential. James writes:

> If any of you lacks wisdom, he should ask God, who gives generously to all without finding fault, and it will be given to him. But when he asks, he must believe and not doubt, because he who doubts is like a wave of the sea, blown and tossed by the wind. That man should not think he will receive anything from the Lord; he is a double-minded man, unstable in all he does. (James 1:5–8)

---

2. Augustine, *Homilia* 43.7, 9.
3. Anselm, *Proslogion* 1.1. The English translation is from Anselm, *Basic Writings*, ed. and trans. Thomas Williams (Indianapolis: Hackett, 2007), 81. At the end of this quotation, Anselm cites the Old Latin version of Isaiah 7:9.

Likewise, because obedience is the fruit of genuine faith (James 2:14–26), God expects his children to walk before him in a manner worthy of their calling (Eph. 4:1). Indeed, if a professed Christian does not have a lifestyle of obedience (and repentance for his failures), his relationship with the Lord will be hindered. A consistently unrepentant lifestyle of sin shows that one's profession of faith is false (1 John 1:6).

Peter warns, "Husbands, in the same way be considerate as you live with your wives, and treat them with respect as the weaker partner and as heirs with you of the gracious gift of life, so that nothing will hinder your prayers" (1 Peter 3:7). A pastor who is unloving and nonsacrificial toward his wife and children can expect little illumination from the Holy Spirit in the study or the pulpit. "Without holiness, no one will see the Lord" (Heb. 12:14), warns the author of Hebrews.[4] Without lives lived in faith and obedience (though certainly full of failure and repentance too; see 1 John 1:8–10), we can expect little divine assistance in understanding and explaining the Scriptures. In fact, when Paul lists the qualifications of pastors, all but one are character qualities—living in integrity before the church and the world (1 Tim. 3:1–7; Titus 1:5–9).[5] The men who explain God's Word to the gathered church must be people who live according to that Word.

After teaching his disciples a model prayer (the Lord's Prayer), Jesus warns, "For if you forgive men when they sin against you, your heavenly Father will also forgive you. But if you do not forgive men their sins, your Father will not forgive your sins" (Matt. 6:14–15). We may be able to recite a systematic theology text from memory, but if our lives are devoid of the love and faith we profess, we are nothing but clanging gongs or clattering cymbals—empty, annoying noisemakers (1 Cor. 13:1).

When Paul begins his letter to Philemon, he writes, "I always thank my God as I remember you in my prayers, because I hear about your faith in the Lord Jesus and your love for all the saints" (Philem. 4–5). Here are the essential prerequisites for biblical study that pleases God—faith in the Lord Jesus and love for others.

---

4. Though the author of Hebrews appears to be referring to one's standing before the Lord at the final judgment, the statement is equally true in this life.
5. The only skill or non-character quality listed is having the ability to teach (1 Tim. 3:2; Titus 1:9).

Do Not Just Affirm Sound Interpretive Principles; Apply Them

At the seminary where I teach, there is a large, grassy lawn in the middle of the campus. Decades ago, two parallel sidewalks ran through the middle of this lawn. Though the sidewalks have been gone for years, in the hot summer months, two brown stripes reappear in the lawn. Why does the grass continue to turn brown? Possibly it is because the dirt was packed underneath the sidewalks, or perhaps it is due to the chemicals used on the sidewalks for weed control. Regardless, the memory of these sidewalks is hard to erase. Similarly, students may come to affirm sound principles of interpretation in a hermeneutics class, but in the heat of regular ministry old patterns continue to surface.

Modern ministers are not the only ones who struggle for consistency in their theoretical and practical hermeneutical methods. Historians of biblical interpretation often note that proponents of sound interpretation throughout church history have failed to consistently apply their own advice. For all his denunciations of allegorical exegesis, Martin Luther sometimes fell prey to it himself.[6] Similarly, Augustine enumerated several helpful principles of exegesis that he did not consistently employ.[7]

A student taking a course in biblical interpretation can get perfect scores on all the tests and assignments and still end up failing to faithfully interpret the Bible in his or her ministry. Once the student is out of the artificial environment of the classroom, he will discover what many ministers have before him, that it is much harder work to prepare a faithful Bible study or sermon than to talk spontaneously about what he thinks people need to hear.

One of the saddest legacies of a ministry that fails to handle God's Word correctly is a congregation that is spiritually starving and confused. Over time, rather than learning how to understand the Bible, a congregation that sits under an unfaithful interpreter will learn how to misinterpret the Bible. As children and grandchildren are affected, potentially hundreds, if not thousands, of people are led into error and spiritual malaise. In considering the

---

6. Robert H. Stein, *The Method and Message of Jesus' Teachings*, rev. ed. (Louisville, KY: Westminster John Knox, 1994), 48.
7. So judges Bernard Ramm, *Protestant Biblical Interpretation: A Textbook of Hermeneutics*, 3rd ed. (Grand Rapids: Baker, 1970), 37.

devastation that one bad preacher can cause, it is little wonder that James warns us, "Not many of you should presume to be teachers, my brothers, because you know that we who teach will be judged more strictly" (James 3:1).

An unfaithful interpreter also can create a spiritual codependency—a situation in which people feel they must come to the pastor to understand the text because they are never able to see on their own the things he emphasizes in his teaching. These poor, starving infants who should have been fed on the pure milk of the Word (1 Peter 2:2) stare with gaunt eyes at the pulpit each week, hoping that manna will fall from heaven.

Welcome and Receive Feedback Graciously

The main teaching pastor at my church has the habit of e-mailing his sermon to five or six trusted friends on Saturday night. We have the responsibility of giving him correction and encouragement on his message. Often, I have little to say, but occasionally my words have kept him from error.

When I first started preaching, I would always ask my wife to read my sermon. Sometimes her criticisms were quite withering, and I did not want to hear them; but after reflection, I usually came around to agree with her.

If you want to know the truth about your teaching—both at the level of interpretation and delivery—you are going to have to ask. And it is likely you are going to have to ask several times and make it clear that you are not going to strike back or hold it against people if they tell you the truth. It is probably best to decide beforehand exactly what you will say. You can rehearse the interchange in your mind. For example, here are some words you can adapt to your setting.

> I'm a bit nervous to ask you this because I know I have room to improve, but I was wondering if you could e-mail me your honest feedback on my sermon. I want to be a more faithful interpreter and better communicator, and I believe you can help me. Please feel free to offer any advice at all. Do not be afraid to offer criticisms. That is what I want.

Also, decide beforehand not to defend yourself. Respond only with thanksgiving—even if you feel that some of the advice was misguided or unjustified. If you seek to defend yourself, do not expect to ever get honest feedback again from the person to whom you are responding.

If you feel sheepish about opening yourself up to criticism from someone in your current setting, possibly you can e-mail your sermon or Bible lesson to an old friend from college or seminary. Ideally, you should move toward asking those in your current setting. Over time, you can develop a trusted cadre of advisers and rejoice to see their interpretive skill developing along with your own. Possibly God will raise up other leaders to share the teaching ministry through these relationships.

As you seek the help of others in growing as an interpreter, here are two proverbs on which to meditate.

- *Proverbs 27:17:* "As iron sharpens iron, so one man sharpens another."

- *Proverbs 24:26:* "An honest answer is like a kiss on the lips."

Acquire and Employ Bible Study Tools

Erasmus, a church leader in the sixteenth century, said, "When I get a little money, I buy books; and if any is left, I buy food and clothes."[8] We can be thankful that we don't live in such lean days, but a diligent student of the Bible will make it a priority to purchase books to aid in his or her study of the Scriptures.

Besides acquiring several modern translations of the Bible (or accessing them via www.biblegateway.com), your first purchase probably should be a good study Bible. A study Bible will not only give you a helpful overview of each book but also provide verse notes to help you understand more obscure statements. The notes in a study Bible obviously will exhibit the doctrinal biases of the persons writing those notes. For that reason, I recommend the *Zondervan NIV Study Bible* and the *ESV Study Bible* (Crossway). Both are respected works whose notes represent the broad consensus of evangelical scholarship. The *Holman Christian Standard Study Bible*, a fine work by Southern Baptist scholars, can be viewed free online at www.mystudybible.com.

---

8. This is Erasmus' supposed quip, as it is often repeated. The closest wording I could locate in his published works reads: "The first thing I shall do, as soon as the money arrives, is to buy some Greek authors; after that, I shall buy clothes" (Letter 124, "To Jacob Batt, Paris, 12 April [1500]," in *The Correspondence of Erasmus, Letters 1 to 141, 1484 to 1500*, trans. R. A. B. Mynors and D. F. S. Thomson [Toronto: University of Toronto Press: 1974], 1:252).

As you continue your study of the Scriptures and are seeking more in-depth study aids, consult chapter 4, "Helpful Books and Tools for Interpreting the Bible."

Pass on What You Are Learning

In the spiritual life, you are either a stagnant pool or a flowing fountain. If you are learning but not sharing what you are learning, you will be like an algae-covered pond. Much of the advice above has assumed that the readers of this book are engaged in or aspire to some public ministry. Possibly you don't see yourself in public ministry. Yet, when it comes to the Bible, all of God's people are to overflow with the truths they are learning. Even if your conversations about the Bible are with your children, spouse, and neighbors, you should be seeking to share the new insights you are learning about God.

REFLECTION QUESTIONS

1. Is reading the Bible your daily practice? If not, why not start today?

2. Is the Bible taught faithfully at your church? Are you and your family being edified and challenged by Scripture there?

3. If you currently teach or preach the Bible, do you have a method for receiving feedback on your teaching?

4. Do you own a study Bible? If so, who is the publisher? What is the stated aim of your study Bible notes?

5. What relationships do you have that allow you to share what you are learning from the Bible?

FOR FURTHER STUDY

ESV Study Bible. Wheaton, IL: Crossway, 2008.
HCSB Study Bible. Nashville, TN: Holman Bible Publishers, 2010.
Zondervan NIV Study Bible. Rev. ed. Edited by Kenneth L. Barker, et
    al. Grand Rapids: Zondervan, 2008.

CHAPTER 4

Helpful Books and Tools for Interpreting the Bible

As a New Testament professor, I am often asked for advice on word study tools and commentaries. Certainly, I am an advocate of having excellent tools to aid in Bible study, but in order to orient ourselves properly before delving into this question, let us begin with two quotes from the Puritan pastor Richard Baxter (1615–1691).

> Make careful choice of the books which you read. *Let the holy Scriptures ever have the pre-eminence*; and, next [to] them, the solid, lively, heavenly treatises, which best expound and apply the Scriptures; and next [to] those, the credible histories, especially of the church . . . but take heed of the poison of the writings of false teachers, which would corrupt your understandings.[1]

> *It is not the reading of many books which is necessary to make a man wise or good; but the well reading of a few,* could he be sure to have the best. And it is not possible to read over very many on the same subjects, without a great deal of loss of precious time.[2]

Two things stand out in these quotes: the preeminence of Scripture and the necessity of having discernment in which books to

---

1. Richard Baxter, "A Christian Directory," part I ("Christian Ethics"), chapter II, Direct XVI, in *The Practical Works of Richard Baxter* (London: George Virtue, 1846; reprint, Morgan, PA: Soli Deo Gloria, 2000), 1:56 (my emphasis).
2. Richard Baxter, "A Christian Directory," part III ("Christian Ecclesiastics"), "Ecclesiastical Cases of Conscience," Question 174, in *The Practical Works of Richard Baxter* (London: George Virtue, 1846; reprint, Morgan, PA: Soli Deo Gloria, 2000), 1:731 (my emphasis).

consult. In this question, we will assume the priority of Scripture and move on to give advice on which particular books to acquire in various categories.

Study Bibles

A study Bible provides extensive notes on the text of Scripture. Such Bibles often advocate a certain theological perspective (e.g., *The Reformation Study Bible*, *The Spirit-Filled Life Study Bible*), or a concern for the questions of a particular demographic subgroup (e.g., *Woman's Study Bible*, *Military Study Bible*), or the investigation of questions from the vantage point of a certain theological discipline (*The Apologetics Study Bible*, *The Archaeological Study Bible*), or the influence of a certain prominent Christian teacher (*The MacArthur Study Bible* [John MacArthur], *The New Inductive Study Bible* [Kay Arthur]). For a young Christian, a study Bible can be very helpful by providing brief summaries and historical backgrounds for each book of the Bible, supplying discussion of difficult and debated texts, and offering cross-references and indices. Wrongly used, a study Bible can provide a crutch that discourages Christians from thinking about and wrestling with texts for themselves. Also, if a person purchases a study Bible from an avowed theological perspective, one faces the danger of letting theological predilections take priority over the text of Scripture.

If you are seeking a study Bible that represents the broad consensus of evangelical scholarship, it is difficult to do much better than *The Zondervan NIV Study Bible* or *The ESV Study Bible*. *The HCSB Study Bible*, an excellent resource produced by Southern Baptist scholars, can be accessed free online at www.mystudybible.com.

Concordances

A concordance is an index for the Bible. An exhaustive concordance lists every occurrence of every word in the Bible. (Yes, even the words *the* and *and*!) Many people who grew up using the King James Version (KJV) are familiar with *Strong's Concordance*, an exhaustive concordance of the KJV compiled by James Strong (1822–1894) and first published in 1890. Concordances are available for all major English Bible translations, and if you purchase a concordance, you should get one for the translation you regularly use. Because of their attempt to consistently translate the underlying Greek or Hebrew words, formally equivalent (word-for-word) translations (for example, the New American Standard Bible or the English Standard Version) are easier to use with a concordance. Properly employed, a concordance allows one not only to find the repetition of the same word in the English translation but also to determine the underlying Greek or Hebrew word. (Greek and Hebrew words are assigned numbers so that those who do not know these languages can trace the repetition of the words throughout Scripture.)

In using a concordance, those with a limited knowledge of linguistics can make wrong assumptions about how to apply their recognition of repeated words. For example, a basic principle of linguistics is that words have a range of meaning and that the immediate context is the most important determiner of meaning. With a concordance, a beginning interpreter could illegitimately force the contextual nuances of a word in one occurrence onto other passages. With appropriate caveats, however, a concordance can be a helpful tool. Any decent Bible software program also will have a search feature that functions like an exhaustive concordance (see below on software programs).

Word Study Tools

Never before in the history of Christianity has there been less need for word studies. With the multiplicity of many excellent modern English Bible translations, readers of the Bible have the fruit of scholars' pains-taking research. At the same time, it is a healthy desire for Christians to want to suck the marrow from every word of Scripture. However, as noted above, an uninformed linguistic euphoria can result in distortions of the text, rather than greater understanding. The following represents two common dangers regarding word studies.

1. *Illegitimate Totality Transfer.* All words have a range of meaning, and the nuances of each particular use cannot be read into all other uses of the word. That is, if the reader takes the totality of what a word *can* mean and reads that potentiality as a reality in every word occurrence, he has illegitimately transferred the totality of what the word means onto each instance (thus, the label "illegitimate totality transfer"). People tolerate erroneous linguistic approaches to the Bible that they would never accept in ordinary speech. For example, imagine the howls one would encounter if he said, "You just used the

word *cell* to describe your phone. By that, I take it that your phone is a small room of incarceration, that your phone is a wireless device, and that your phone is a microscopic blob of protoplasm." Obviously, only one of the potential meanings of "cell" is intended. Yet, how many times have we heard a similar litany of potential meanings from a preacher presented as "the real meaning" of a word in the Bible? One can see the danger of tools like *The Amplified Bible,* which provides several possible meanings of most words. Without further instruction, such tools lead one down the path of illegitimate totality transfer.

2. *Etymological Fallacy.* Etymology is the study of the ancestry of words. Thus, the etymological fallacy is to wrongly believe that knowing the history of a word gives us deeper insight into its current meaning. There have been periods in biblical scholarship when even well-trained scholars were taken in by the siren song of etymology. More commonly, in popular preaching, one hears the etymology of a word sometimes given as "what this word really means." To illustrate the foolishness of the etymological fallacy to my classes, I give examples from the English language. For example:

- When you hear the word *tuxedo,* undoubtedly, you think of the Algonquian Indian word for "wolf," from which the word *tuxedo* was derived. Unconsciously, you almost hear yourself saying, "There goes that dapper wolf!"

- When your neighbor speaks of spraying herbicide on dandelions in his yard, you think about the underlying French words *dent de lion* ("tooth of the lion"). You might ask, "Those roaring weeds are sinking their sharp incisors into your lawn again, eh?"

- Your wife says that she is cooking lasagna for supper. You can't help recalling that the word *lasagna* ultimately derives from the Greek term for "chamber potty" (*lasonon*). "Going to dish us up another one from the toilet?" you innocently ask.

The reality is that words mean what the writers intended for them to mean in the historical context in which they were written. The ordinary use of language (a word's potential range of meaning) constrains the possible meanings unless the author clearly points out that he is using a word differently from the way it would normally be understood. Thus, in the early twenty-first century, to say that someone is wearing "gay clothing" (without further qualification) means something quite different from what it meant when the translators of the KJV chose that expression when translating James 2:3 in the early seventeenth century.

In spite of all these warnings against the misuse of word studies, they can be helpful in clarifying the nuances of important words. In the case of a very rare word where we have few or no other instances of the word in the same time period, it can be legitimate to appeal to etymology to help us determine its meaning. Also, proper names (the names of people or places) often are presented in Scripture as informed by their etymology.[3] The most reliable and accessible word study tool for those lacking knowledge of Greek and Hebrew may be *Mounce's Complete Expository Dictionary of Old and New Testament Words*. For more detail, see *The New International Dictionary of Old Testament Theology and Exegesis* and *The New International Dictionary of New Testament Theology*.

Commentaries

Commentaries are books that explain the text of Scripture, usually in a verse-by-verse or paragraph-by-paragraph method. There are one-volume commentaries on the whole Bible,[4] but the most extensive and thoughtful reflections on Scripture can be found in monographs devoted to individual books of the Bible. Individual commentaries also sometimes focus on a few related books, such as the Johannine Epistles (1, 2, and 3 John) or the Pastoral Epistles (1 and 2 Timothy, Titus).

If one were to teach through Romans, the careful teacher should obtain several good commentaries on Romans to read in his weekly

---

3. See Robert H. Stein, *A Basic Guide to Interpreting the Bible: Playing by the Rules* (Grand Rapids: Baker, 1994), 173.

4. One of the best one-volume Bible commentaries is *The New Bible Commentary: 21st Century Edition*, ed. G. J. Wenham, J. A. Motyer, D. A. Carson, and R. T. France (Downers Grove, IL: InterVarsity Press, 1994).

preparation. At their best, commentaries function as a virtual community of other believers dialoguing with the teacher about the text. A Christian teacher was not meant to function in isolation or to refuse the beneficial input of other Spirit-gifted teachers in the church. At the most fundamental level, a commentary guards a teacher from idiosyncratic interpretations. Indeed, if you are the only person to understand a biblical passage in a certain way, you are almost certainly wrong.

A number of caveats about commentaries should be noted.

1. Pastors or diligent laypersons are sometimes eager to obtain a complete commentary series, that is, a set produced under the same series title by one publisher. While such a commentary set looks nice with the matching dust jackets on one's shelf (and gives the air of erudition to the owner), it is better to purchase individual volumes based on the quality of the scholarship. Commentaries within the same series can vary greatly in quality. Money spent to acquire mediocre or poor work is money wasted. I own several complete commentary series, but they were all acquired at a great discount.

2. Studious Christians often are attracted to software programs that promise hundreds of commentaries and/or the ability to acquire other commentaries electronically. Nevertheless, if one does not currently prefer to read books in digital format, he should be forewarned of spending money to buy a digital library. Moreover, many of the titles that come as standard on some Bible software programs are volumes already in the public domain (likely available as free downloads on Web sites) or works of limited scholarly value. To truly get the best commentaries, one will usually have to pay—whether for a digital copy or bound book. I do have one complete Bible commentary series loaded onto the hard drive of my laptop computer, *The Expositor's Bible Commentary* (Zondervan). This set also comes in hard copy as thirteen volumes (revised ed., 2010). I like having this series in digital format for two reasons. First, when I am traveling with my computer, I am sure to have access to at least one generally helpful commentary on any book of the Bible. Second, in giving quick replies to e-mails about particular passages of the Bible, I sometimes

save time by pasting in a portion of the commentary (with adequate citation, of course).

3. Christians are advised to build their libraries slowly and thoughtfully. Every time you begin the detailed study of a new book in the Bible, you should consult one of two guidebooks to determine which individual commentaries to purchase: Tremper Longman's *Old Testament Commentary Survey* or D. A. Carson's *New Testament Commentary Survey*.[5] These texts are filled with excellent advice and are also worth skimming in their entirety for their more general suggestions on acquiring and using commentaries. Less detailed but free advice is available at www.bestcommentaries.com.

4. Many pastors and professors have bookshelves full of tomes they have never read and never will read. Money to acquire books you will never read is better spent on more productive things. There are many ways to acquire needed books in an affordable fashion. Be creative and diligent. You will prize the fruit of your frugality.

Software Programs

Software programs are helpful for studying the Bible in two areas:

1. *Navigating the text of the Bible.* If you have some training in Greek or Hebrew, software programs have some incredible, time-saving features—linking lexicons, diagramming the texts, allowing morphological searches, etc. In my opinion, the best programs are Bibleworks (my personal favorite), Accordance (for Mac users), Logos/Libronix, and Gramcord. If you cannot use Greek or Hebrew but want software to search the English text, possibly a free program like E-sword would suffice (see www.e-sword.net). For accessing Bibles or

---

5. Tremper Longman, *Old Testament Commentary Survey*, 4th ed. (Grand Rapids: Baker, 2007); and D. A. Carson, *New Testament Commentary Survey*, 6th ed. (Grand Rapids: Baker, 2007). Also see John Glynn, *Commentary and Reference Survey: A Comprehensive Guide to Biblical and Theological Resources*, 10th ed. (Grand Rapids: Kregel, 2007).

reference works on my smart phone, I've found no better platform than Olive Tree's BibleReader app.

2. *Providing helpful secondary texts.* Personally, I prefer bound volumes, but if you are a reader of digital books, the best software for a digital library is Logos/Libronix. With the plethora of e-readers now available (Amazon's Kindle, Barnes and Noble's Nook, the iPad, etc.) purchasers of digital texts have many viewing options at their disposal.

Web Sites

Without endorsing all their content, a few Web sites I have found helpful for biblical and theological research are:

- www.biblegateway.com: to look up verses and compare Bible translations.

- www.bible.org: for a variety of biblical and theological resources.

- www.desiringgod.org: John Piper's ministry Web site, with a variety of resources available.

- www.fpcjackson.org: for accessing hundreds of Ligon Duncan's sermon manuscripts.

- www.monergism.com: for resources from a Calvinistic perspective.

- www.theopedia.com: Wikipedia (online encyclopedia) for theology.

- www.equip.org: apologetics Web site run by "The Bible Answer Man," Hank Hanegraaff.

- www.watchman.org: an anti-cult Web site.

- www.4truth.net: apologetics Web site run by the North American Mission Board of the Southern Baptist Convention.

- www.ntgateway.com: a "scholarly index" for Web sites related to the New Testament.

- www.greekbible.com: for accessing the Greek New Testament with vocabulary and parsing helps.

- www.biblicalfoundations.org: helpful biblical reflections by New Testament scholar Andreas Köstenberger.

The amount of material available at the click of a mouse is nearly intoxicating. The wisdom of digested truth, however, is harder to find. The neophyte theologian must beware the dangers of plagiarism, superficial reading, and repeating the mistakes and misunderstandings of others.

Advanced Study

As one grows in skill as an interpreter of the Bible, he will also desire to study in other areas, such as systematic theology, practical ministry, church history, missiology, etc. Christian classics (works of a previous generation) should not be neglected; there is a reason such works have survived. Reading a modern summary of a classic text never compares with ruminating on the original. One springboard to more advanced study is to listen to one of the many high-quality audio lectures by leading evangelical scholars at the following two Web sites: www.biblicaltraining.org and www.worldwide-classroom.com.

REFLECTION QUESTIONS

1. What tools, besides a Bible, do you currently use in your study of Scripture?

2. Do you own any useful Bible study tools that you are failing to use? Why?

3. Of the resources discussed above, what are the top ones on your wish list of future acquisitions?

4. Have you ever engaged in any of the word study fallacies discussed above? Do you feel that you sufficiently understand the fallacies to avoid them in the future?

5. If someone were to ask you, "What book can you recommend to help me understand Ecclesiastes?" where would you go for trustworthy advice on relevant resources?

FOR FURTHER STUDY

BibleWorks Version 9.0: Software for Biblical Exegesis and Research. BibleWorks, LLC. 2009. See www.bibleworks.com.

Brown, Colin., ed. *New International Dictionary of New Testament Theology.* 4 vols. Grand Rapids: Zondervan, 1975, 1986.

Carson, D. A. *Exegetical Fallacies.* Grand Rapids: Baker, 1984 (See "Word-Study Fallacies," 25–66).

_____. *New Testament Commentary Survey.* 6th ed. Grand Rapids: Baker, 2007.

Glynn, John. *Commentary and Reference Survey: A Comprehensive Guide to Biblical and Theological Resources.* 10th ed. Grand Rapids: Kregel, 2007.

Longman, Tremper. *Old Testament Commentary Survey.* 4th ed. Grand Rapids: Baker, 2007.

Mounce, William D., ed. *Mounce's Complete Expository Dictionary of Old and New Testament Words.* Grand Rapids: Zondervan, 2006.

VanGemeren, Willem A., ed. *New International Dictionary of Old Testament Theology and Exegesis.* 5 vols. Grand Rapids: Zondervan, 1997.

CHAPTER 5

Determining the Meaning of a Biblical Text

In any act of communication (a speech, conversation, handwritten letter, or e-mail), there are three elements: a writer or speaker, a text or spoken words, and a reader or listener.[1] In what way do these different parts of the communication process affect or determine meaning? Who or what is the final arbiter of meaning, assuming there is such an arbiter? Scholars reach highly divergent conclusions to these questions. We will survey the main approaches below, arguing for the author as the ultimate determiner of meaning.

The Reader as Determiner of Meaning

The dominant approach in the secular academy to interpreting literature highlights the reader as the ultimate determiner of meaning. According to this approach, even if the author were to stand up and say, "That's not what I meant," the reader would respond, "Who cares what you meant? This is the meaning *for me*." Such a reader-determined meaning is sometimes also called a reader-response approach to literature. (That is, each reader responds to the literature in the creation of meaning.) These reader-created meanings are at times self-consciously driven by various philosophical or social concerns (e.g., the Marxist reading, the feminist reading, the homosexual reading, the environmentalist reading, the liberationist reading). Other times, the reader may simply appeal to his or her idiosyncratic view

---

1. Of course, this is the main paradigm of communication, but there are related permutations—for example, with two deaf persons there would be a signer, the signs used, and the viewer of the signs. Or, with spies, there might be an encoder, the code used, and the decoder.

without any reference to a broader social agenda. We should note that the reader-response approach to literature is *not* the reader discovering the author's meaning or the application of the authorial meaning in the reader's life. The reader is the actual determiner or creator of meaning, with the exclusion of any external judge.[2]

Such an interpretive approach, of course, inevitably results in readers proposing a variety of contradictory meanings. Adherents of the reader-response approach to literature would rather affirm various irreconcilable interpretations than suggest that one interpretation is more valid than another. A rejection of absolutist statements underlies the reader-response approach. An unwelcome sentence begins: "*The* meaning of this text is . . ." Permissible is: "*To me*, this text means . . ." In a pluralistic and multicultural society, it is seen as arrogant to claim final legitimacy for only one interpretation or opinion.

Another issue often underlying the reader-response approach to literature is the assumption that language is an instrument of oppression or liberation.[3] That is, texts are primarily used to assert power rather than to convey and receive information. While it is true that texts, including the Bible, do bring about action and change, one must be quite cynical to reduce the reading and writing of texts to underhanded power plays.

As modern America is imbued by the reader-response approach to literature and the assumptions that underlie it, it is difficult not to be influenced by it. In fact, many self-proclaimed Christian writers and scholars have adopted the reader-response approach in much the same way the early church adopted the allegorical approach of the surrounding Greco-Roman culture. I will offer two examples of the reader-response approach to the Bible from my everyday experiences.

---

2. Robin Parry offers this helpful caveat: "Reader-response theory is not a single theory but a family of diverse hermeneutical theories that share a focus on the *active role* of the reader (or communities of readers) in interpretation. The various theorists disagree on a range of issues: how much control texts exercise in interpretation, the role of communities within which readers live, the role of the interpretive histories of texts, whether the readers they speak of are experts or ordinary readers, and so on" ("Reader-Response Criticism," in *Dictionary for Theological Interpretation of the Bible*, ed. Kevin J. Vanhoozer [Grand Rapids: Baker; London: SPCK, 2005], 658–59).

3. Technically, this assumption belongs more to deconstructionism, but the approaches overlap.

1. In a children's Bible that was given to my daughter, the story of Joseph is followed by these questions: "Has anyone ever given you something like a new coat or sweater? How did it make you feel to put on the new clothes?"[4] It is clear that the author of this children's Bible values self-esteem and affirmation. Even though the writer of the biblical text obviously is not relating the story of Joseph to cause sentimental reflection on how others have affirmed us, the modern author of the children's Bible has used the story for this purpose. He or she has created meaning alien to the biblical author's intent. The issue is not whether the interpreter's point is valid (that is, encouraging sentimental reflections to build self-esteem). The issue is: what was the purpose, intent, or meaning of the inspired biblical author?

2. A while back, my wife and I met with a lady who had recently come to saving faith through a parachurch ministry but was still attending a largely unregenerate mainline church. She was puzzled because her pastor preached from Matthew 13:24–30 (the parable of the wheat and the weeds), encouraging parishioners to remove the weeds from their lives and tend the wheat. "But," the lady said in consternation, "when I look in my Bible, Jesus himself explains the parable and says the weeds are wicked people who are cast into hell!" (Matt. 13:37–43). The pastor at this lady's church likely found the doctrine of hell offensive, so he reinterpreted the parable to offer a more palatable message.

The Text as Determiner of Meaning

Another approach to communication that was popular in literary circles from the 1930s to the 1960s is to look to the text as the determiner of meaning.[5] Unlike the reader-response approach, the text-de-

---

4. These are the questions as I recall them. We did not keep the Bible.
5. This interpretive approach is called the new criticism or Formalism. Michael E. Travers notes, "Philosophically, modern versions of formalism developed out of Immanuel Kant and aesthetically from the Romantic poets of the early nineteenth century. . . . In the United States, formalism received its classic expression in the New Criticism of the mid-twentieth century, in the works of such writers as Cleanth Brooks, John Crowe Ransom, Robert Penn Warren, and William Wimsatt. The term 'New Criticism' is to be understood in the context of their

termined approach does accept an objective arbiter of meaning, but it is not the author. After the author finishes his work, the text is viewed as taking on a life of its own—containing meanings beyond the intent, and possibly contrary to the desire of, the original composer. Thus, knowing the historical setting and original addressees of a document is of no importance, according to this approach.

It is necessary to point out a few potential misunderstandings of the text-determined approach to meaning. First, most people who state, "The Bible says" are not advocating the text-determined approach to meaning. In saying, "The Bible says," the speaker usually means the same thing as, "The inspired biblical author says." Second, the text-determined view should not be confused with the normal interpretive process of proposing implications that go beyond the conscious thought of the author. For example, in Proverbs 23:10, the inspired author forbids stealing of a neighbor's property through moving boundary stones. By implication, any other underhanded method to defraud your neighbor of his property is also forbidden. Though the ancient author of Proverbs was not thinking about the falsification of a land survey using a computer scanner, surely such behavior is also forbidden by implication. Such implications flow within the channel of meaning intended by the author at the time of his original composition.

A major criticism of text-determined meaning is that texts are inanimate objects—ink on paper, or scratches on stone.[6] Meaning, on the other hand, is a construction of intelligent thought. Texts can convey meaning, but texts cannot construct meaning. Constructing meaning is the role of the author. Meaning, ultimately then, lies in the purview of the author.

The Author as Determiner of Meaning

The final theory of communication (and the one I am advocating) is that the author of a text is the ultimate arbiter of its meaning.[7] Thus, as much as possible, it is important to study the historical setting and

---

wish to move past the historical and biographical study of literature in American university classrooms of the day to a literary criticism that is more text-based" ("Formalism," in *Dictionary for Theological Interpretation of the Bible*, 230).

6. Robert H. Stein, "The Benefits of an Author-Oriented Approach to Hermeneutics," *Journal of the Evangelical Theological Society* 44, no. 3 (2001): 53.

7. E. D. Hirsch, *Validity in Interpretation* (New Haven, CT: Yale University Press, 1967).

original addressee(s) of a document to understand better the author's intent and purpose in writing. At times, it may be difficult to determine the author's meaning, but that is the goal that all valid interpretation seeks. The role of the reader of a text, then, is to discover the author's consciously intended meaning.

One of the main arguments for the author-determined approach to meaning is that this method is the commonsense approach to all communication. If your friend says, "I would like a hamburger for lunch," and you respond, "Why is it that you hate Caucasians?" the person would rightly respond, "Are you crazy? Did you not hear what I said?" Any act of communication can progress only on the assumption that someone is trying to convey meaning to us and we then respond to that meaning intended by the speaker or writer.

Objections to the Author as Determiner of Meaning

Below is a list of objections to the author as determiner of meaning, with responses following.

1. *We can never access the author's thoughts, so the authorial meaning of the text is inaccessible to us.*[8] It is true that we can never access the private thoughts of an author. Right now, as I am typing on my computer keyboard, am I ambivalent or engaged in writing this book? Am I motivated by duty, devotion, or a desire for money or fame? You will never know. But, unless I am an incompetent writer, you are able to understand the meaning and intent of my writing. The multitude of thoughts and feelings I have while writing this book are of no import to the actual intent of my communication.[9] To seek the author's meaning is not to seek his private thoughts or feelings.

---

8. William K. Wimsatt Jr. and Monroe C. Beardsley, "The Intentional Fallacy," *Sewanee Review* 54 (1946): 468–88. Hirsch writes, "The argument that an interpreter's understanding is necessarily different because he is different assumes a psychologistic conception of meaning which mistakenly identifies meaning with mental processes rather than with an object of those processes" (*Validity in Interpretation*, 32).

9. A point made well by C. S. Lewis in his essay, "Fern-seed and Elephants," in *Fern-seed and Elephants and Other Essays on Christianity by C. S. Lewis*, ed. Walter Hooper (London: Fontana/Collins, 1975), 104–25. I must thank Robert Stein for introducing me to this essay.

2. *An author's worldview might be so distant from our own that we can never claim to understand his meaning.*[10] This criticism might especially be offered for the Bible, where the most recent of its works is nearly two thousand years old. What this criticism fails to recognize, however, is the common nature shared by all human persons. As creatures in the image of God, humans are never so culturally different from each other that understanding is impossible. Cultures and times vary, but the rational human intellect is able to perceive and explain those differences.

3. *To seek the author's intended meaning makes the document irrelevant for modern readers.* This criticism fails to understand the relationship between meaning and implications. The meaning is the original, author-intended purpose of the document. The implications are those modern-day applications of the authorial principle in changing times and cultures. Defining clearly the authorial meaning creates a channel in which the interpreter's implications can safely flow.

4. *To delimit meaning to the conscious intent of the human author is to deny the divine authorship of Scripture.* Two responses can be offered to this criticism. First, for the vast majority of Scripture, the conscious human author's meaning and the divinely intended meaning are indistinguishable. When Paul said, "Do everything without complaining or arguing" (Phil. 2:14), one cannot imagine a difference between divine and human authorial intent.

   Second, the problem of distinguishing human and divine intent arises only in prophecy texts, especially those few texts that seem to be used in ways that vary from the human author's explicitly distinguishable original intent. For example, Matthew 2:15 cites Hosea 11:1 with reference to Jesus' return from Egypt. In Hosea, however, the context seems to be referring only to Israel's exodus out of Egypt (as a paradigm

---

10. Hirsch writes, "Only the absolute form of radical historicism threatens the enterprise of re-cognitive interpretation by holding that the meanings of the past are intrinsically alien to us, that we have no 'authentic' access to those meanings and therefore can never 'truly' understand them" (*Validity in Interpretation*, 40).

applied to the Assyrian exile in Hosea's day). Such quotations of the Old Testament by New Testament authors provide the greatest challenge for maintaining the original human composer as the ultimate determiner of a text's meaning. I would argue, however, that divine intent can and should be subsumed under an author-oriented approach to interpreting the Bible. The human authors of Scripture shared an understanding that they were on a salvation-historical trajectory that would climax in the coming of Messiah. God intervened savingly in history in repeated and progressively climactic ways. Old Testament writers who picked up earlier divine interventions to understand their own day (for example, Hosea's allusion to the Egyptian exodus [Hos. 11:1]) implicitly allow for later authors to propose a future divine intervention as the climactic counterpart to their own day. Biblical authors were conscious of being part of a larger divine story and expected later chapters to build upon and escalate what they had already related. For more discussion of this type of biblical prophecy, see the article, "Righteousness and Peace Kiss: The Reconciliation of Authorial Intent and Biblical Typology," available free under the "Resources" tab at www.robplummer.com.

A Vocabulary for Interpretation

Confusion in discussing "meaning" can be caused by those who use the same word in different ways. For example, someone might speak of the "meanings" of the text, but in reality, he is referring to modern-day implications. As we think in more detail about whether a text can have multiple meanings, it is important to begin by clarifying our terms.

In teaching biblical interpretation to seminary students, I begin by defining basic terms that we use repeatedly over the course of the semester. Below are some important terms for interpretation with definitions drawn from Robert Stein.

- *Meaning:* "The paradigm or principle that the author consciously willed to convey by the shareable symbols [i.e., writing] he or she used."[11]

---

11. Robert H. Stein, "The Benefits of an Author-Oriented Approach to Hermeneutics," 457.

- *Implication:* "Those submeanings of a text that legitimately fall within the paradigm or principle willed by the author, whether he or she was aware of them or not."[12]

- *Significance:* "How the reader responds to the willed meaning of the author."[13] Upon being confronted with these implications, the modern-day reader/hearer will then respond with acceptance (obedience) or rejection (disobedience).

- *Subject Matter:* "The content or 'stuff' talked about in the text" (that is, the textual details in and of themselves without reference to their use in conveying the author's meaning).[14]

We can illustrate these terms by looking at a sample text. Let us consider Proverbs 11:1: "The LORD abhors dishonest scales, but accurate weights are his delight." What is the meaning of this text? The author intends to teach his readers that God is pleased when one uses honestly weighted scales in business transactions, and thus the readers should use such scales. Likewise, God is displeased when one uses skewed scales to cheat others. The readers of this proverb are implicitly warned not to engage in such trickery. The author's original meaning, likely made with reference to the measuring of precious metals or agricultural produce, is clear.

What are the implications? Depending on the setting of the modern-day reader, a variety of implications are possible. The implications must flow within the channel of meaning determined by the conscious intent of the author; they must be "submeanings" of the original paradigm. For example, an hourly worker who punches in and out on a time clock can say, by implication, that God is pleased when he honestly clocks in and out as he comes and goes from work. Likewise, God is displeased with the worker who has his friends clock him out ten minutes after he has already left (so that he is paid for additional time for which he did not work). When hearing these implications declared, the hourly worker will then respond with obedience or disobedience (in Stein's terminology, significance).The writer of Proverbs clearly was not thinking of a time clock, but the paradigm

---

12. Ibid., 458.
13. Ibid., 460.
14. Ibid., 461.

of honest and dishonest business practices has many modern-day implications of which the author was not consciously aware. If the original author were consulted (obviously only a hypothetical possibility), he should agree that the modern-day implications flow legitimately from his meaning. The original author is the determiner of meaning, which in turn, limits implications. Sometimes, it can be helpful to imagine a dialogue with the original author over proposed implications in an attempt to make sure they flow directly from the author's consciously intended purpose. No modern-day implication, however, is complete without reference to Christ. No matter how honest we are, the apostle Paul's indictment falls on us: "There is no one righteous, not even one" (Rom. 3:10). Compared to God's holy standard, we are all deceivers in need of the forgiveness and grace found in Jesus Christ.

What about the "subject matter" in Proverbs 11:1? The "scales" and "weights" (the "stuff" mentioned in the text) are examples of subject matter. In and of themselves, scales and weights are not the purpose of the author's instruction. One can imagine a misguided preacher going into great detail on the composition of ancient weights and the construction of ancient scales. Neither issue, however, is of real import to the author's meaning (that is, honesty in business transactions). Scales and weights in and of themselves are not the meaning of the text, but the author of Proverbs mentions them to convey a teaching about honesty with reference to the original readers' regular activities. The subject matter is essential for conveying meaning but does not contain meaning in and of itself without regard to the author's purpose.

Challenging Texts and Multiple Meanings

The text chosen above (Prov. 11:1) is relatively straightforward, but what about more difficult texts—texts that later biblical authors seem to infuse with additional meaning beyond the conscious intent of the original authors? Let's consider such a text and various ways of interpreting it.

In Isaiah 7:14, we read, "Therefore the Lord himself will give you a sign: The virgin will be with child and will give birth to a son, and will call him Immanuel." In the original context, this text refers to a child who would be born to "the prophetess" as a sign to King Ahaz of Judah, who reigned from 732 to 716 B.C. Isaiah says that before the promised child is a few years old, Ahaz's adversaries (the kings of Aram and Israel) will be defeated by Assyria (Isa. 7:11–17; 8:1–4). More than seven hundred years later, Matthew quotes Isaiah 7:14 as fulfilled in the birth of Jesus (Matt. 1:23). How can Isaiah's text legitimately apply to both his own day (722 B.C.) and Matthew's day (ca. 4 B.C.)? Below are several possible approaches.

1. One approach to this challenging text is to assert that Matthew has misunderstood and/or illegitimately used Isaiah 7:14. That is, Matthew haphazardly quoted the text without reference to Isaiah's original intent. While some non-Christian scholars take this view, Christians should not consider this a valid option, as Matthew was divinely inspired and would not illegitimately quote the Old Testament (2 Tim. 3:16). Moreover, how likely is it that the author of one of the most beautiful and influential works ever written was incompetent or deceptive? As a Jew writing to Jews who knew the Hebrew Scriptures, Matthew could not afford to be sloppy in his quotations from the Old Testament.

2. Another approach to Isaiah 7:14 claims that the Holy Spirit had an additional hidden meaning for Isaiah's prophecy. Isaiah was not cognizant of a later fulfillment, but the Spirit-inspired author, Matthew, applied the text to Jesus in his day—showing that God had a fuller, deeper sense to the original prophecy, which he revealed at a later time. This later meaning is called the *sensus plenior* (Latin: "fuller sense"). The *sensus plenior* interpretive approach appeals to secret, divine intent as the trump card explanation, seeing no need to justify later usage from the original context. Yet, if an Old Testament text is to be legitimately applied to Jesus, it seems only natural to expect the original human author to have consciously intended that usage on some level.

3. Robert Stein has proposed that we understand difficult texts such as Matthew 1:23 as implications of the original text. That is, Matthew's use is not the original meaning of Isaiah 7:14 but a submeaning of the text that legitimately falls within the principle willed by the author. To my knowledge, Stein has not commented on this specific text in writing, yet he would likely

argue like this: "In the original setting, Ahaz faced certain destruction at the hands of his enemies. God gave the sign of an impending birth to signify the coming divine deliverance. In Matthew's day, with the even greater enemies of death and sin facing God's people (as they had for so long), God does not leave them without ultimate deliverance but signifies his coming climactic intervention in a supernaturally born child." In the end, however, because of the historical particularity of the original prophecy in Isaiah, it seems difficult to explain Matthew's usage as an implication. How can there be an implication for a singularly promised event that has long ago been fulfilled?

4. Another approach for difficult texts like this is to understand that Matthew is employing Isaiah 7:14 typologically. The Old Testament authors shared the understanding that God intervened progressively and repeatedly, working toward a final climactic intervention. Old Testament authors saw deliverance in their day as foreshadowed in God's earlier deliverances. By their reference to earlier divine interventions to explain God's work in their own day and their anticipation of greater deliverance in the future, the Old Testament authors implicitly agree to the future typological use of their own writings.[15] So, if we could go back in time to just after Isaiah penned chapter 7, verse 14 (reporting the prophet's earlier interchange with Ahaz), the dialogue might go like this:

Plummer: "Pardon me, Isaiah. I'm from the distant future, and I've come back to chat with you. I was peeking over your shoulder, and I just noticed that you wrote that prophecy down about the promised child. Is that about Jesus?"

Isaiah: "Who is Jesus?"

Plummer: "Jesus is the coming Messiah who conquers sin and death forever."

15. Jared M. Compton advocates a similar approach ("Shared Intentions? Reflections on Inspiration and Interpretation in Light of Scripture's Dual Authorship," *Themelios* 33, no. 3 [2008]: 23–33).

Isaiah: "Hallelujah! I didn't know his name, but I knew he was coming. What do you mean by asking, 'Is this text about Jesus?'"

Plummer: "Well, in the future, before the Messiah is born, God promises through his angel that a virgin will give birth, similar to the events in your day. Matthew, one of God's messengers in Jesus' day, says that this text of yours was pointing to the Messiah."

Isaiah: "Yes, I see. Just as God signified his coming intervention with the supernatural birth of a child in my day, so in the final deliverance, again he promises the supernatural birth of a child. The historical parallels show God's consistent intentions! Of course, not knowing exactly how God would repeat his deliverance, I was not fully conscious of the final typological correspondence until you told me. But, I knew later deliverances were coming. I wrote this text, consciously knowing it might be reiterated in a later, parallel, heightened saving event. Yes, yes, of course that is a valid use. That's what is called biblical typology, with a correspondence between earlier events (the type[s]) and later events (the antitype[s])."

Plummer: "Thanks for talking with us, Isaiah."

Isaiah: "Shalom."

While I think the typological approach is likely the best way to explain Matthew's usage of Isaiah 7:14, this text in particular has some additional characteristics that are worth noting. One could argue that Isaiah intended multiple references in his original prophecy. That is, Isaiah consciously intended the "virgin prophecy" of Isaiah 7:14 to be applied to the setting in his own day, as well as to some other promised child in the distant future.

What details might indicate that Isaiah has in mind another child beyond the one who will be a sign to King Ahaz in his day? There are, in fact, several descriptions of the child in the immediate context that seem to point beyond anything that was fulfilled by the child in

Ahaz's day. For example, soon after our debated text, in Isaiah 9:6–7, we read:

> For to us a child is born, to us a son is given, and the government will be on his shoulders. And he will be called Wonderful Counselor, Mighty God, Everlasting Father, Prince of Peace. Of the increase of his government and peace there will be no end. He will reign on David's throne and over his kingdom, establishing and upholding it with justice and righteousness from that time on and forever. The zeal of the LORD Almighty will accomplish this.

Such an exalted description certainly would be odd for Maher-Shalal-Hash-Baz (Isaiah's son?), the child in Ahaz's day who makes no additional appearances in the biblical text (Isa. 8:1–4). Furthermore, in Isaiah 8:18, the prophet writes, "Here I am, and the *children* the LORD has given me. We are *signs* and *symbols* in Israel from the LORD Almighty, who dwells on Mount Zion" (my emphasis). It is interesting that the original child-sign (singular) has been broadened out here to refer to "children," "signs," and "symbols"—all plural.

It is possible that Isaiah had a prophetic vision of two children in much the same way that we see two mountains from a distance. Viewed from far away, the two mountains appear side by side as one monolithic structure. One cannot tell how far apart they are or even if they are distinct formations. Only as we draw closer to the initial mountain do we see that the other mountain is actually separated from it by some distance. Similarly, it has been argued, some ancient prophets had visions of multiple forthcoming events in such a way that they could not distinguish the chronological distance between them. The technical term for a variety of future events being viewed together (without strict chronological sequencing) is *prophetic foreshortening*. It has been pointed out that the first and second comings of Jesus are described in the Old Testament with prophetic foreshortening. That is, only with the completion of the first coming of Jesus are we able to see clearly that the Messiah's visible and universal reign (the consummated kingdom) will come after a gap of time.

REFLECTION QUESTIONS

1. In your opinion, why is the reader-response approach to literature so popular at the current time?

2. Of the four objections to the author as the determiner of meaning presented above, which seems to have the most validity to you? Why?

3. Is the distinction between meaning and implications clear to you? Explain the difference in your own words.

4. Refer to Ephesians 5:18, discuss meaning, implications, significance, and subject matter.

5. Which of the four approaches to Isaiah 7:14 seems the most convincing to you?

FOR FURTHER STUDY

Hirsch, E. D. *Validity in Interpretation.* New Haven, CT: Yale University Press, 1967.

Köstenberger, Andreas J. and Richard D. Patterson. *Biblical Interpretation: Exploring the Hermeneutical Triad of History, Literature, and Theology.* Grand Rapids: Kregel, 2011.

Stein, Robert H. *A Basic Guide to Interpreting the Bible: Playing by the Rules.* 2nd ed. Grand Rapids: Baker, 2011. (See chap. 2, "Defining the Rules: A Vocabulary for Interpretation.")

Virkler, Henry A., and Karelynne Gerber Ayayo. *Hermeneutics: Principles and Processes of Biblical Interpretation.* 2nd ed. Grand Rapids: Baker, 2007.

CHAPTER 6

The Role of the Holy Spirit in Interpreting the Bible

As Christians study and talk about the Bible, it is not uncommon for some to appeal to the Holy Spirit's supernatural guidance in determining the meaning or application of a text. Does the Bible, in fact, present the Holy Spirit as working in this way? That is, does the Spirit guide believers to a true meaning or application of the biblical text?

The Person and Work of the Holy Spirit

Before we look at the role of the Holy Spirit in interpretation, we must be clear about the identity of the Spirit. Who is the Holy Spirit? The Holy Spirit is the third person of the triune God. According to Scripture, God is Father, Son, and Spirit (Matt. 28:19)—three distinct "persons" in one Being.[1] The Father is God. The Son is God. The Spirit is God. But there is only one God. And the Father is not the Son, nor is the Spirit the Son, nor is the Father the Spirit. Yet with regard to their divine nature, the Father, Son, and Spirit share the same goodness, wisdom, holiness, knowledge, and power.[2]

The Holy Spirit is sent by the Father and the Son into the world (John 14:26; 15:26). He indwells all true followers of Jesus (Rom. 8:9; 1 John 2:20) and enables them to live in repentance and faith (Rom.

---

1. Although *person* is the word that Christian theologians have traditionally used to refer to the Father, Son, and Spirit, we must note that divine personhood and human personhood differ. A human person has a distinct intellect, background, perspective, etc. The divine persons of the Trinity, however, share exactly the same divine attributes (wisdom, holiness, etc.).

2. For further reflection on the Trinity, see Wayne Grudem, *Systematic Theology: An Introduction to Biblical Doctrine* (Grand Rapids: Zondervan; Leicester: Inter-Varsity Press, 1994), 226–61.

8:1–17). The Holy Spirit empowers God's people with spiritual gifts for the building up of Christ's body, the church (Eph. 4:11–16; 1 Cor. 12:4–11). Furthermore, the Spirit intercedes on behalf of God's people (Rom. 8:26) and reminds us of our filial status (Rom. 8:15; Gal. 4:6).

The Holy Spirit inspired the authors of Scripture so that every word they wrote, while inscribed by a thinking, human author, was also divinely inspired and free from all error. As Peter notes, "[No] prophecy of Scripture came about by the prophet's own interpretation. For prophecy never had its origin in the will of man, but men spoke from God as they were carried along by the Holy Spirit" (2 Peter 1:20–21). Paul likewise writes, "All Scripture is God-breathed and is useful for teaching, rebuking, correcting and training in righteousness" (2 Tim. 3:16). After Jesus' ascension, the Spirit reminded the apostles of the Lord's teaching and taught them further things, which, when written, resulted in our New Testament (John 14:25–26; 16:13–15).

There can be little doubt that the Bible presents itself as the product of the Spirit's inspiration, but does the Bible also present the Spirit as giving believers special aid in understanding its contents?

The Illumination of the Holy Spirit

Most Protestant theologians affirm that the Holy Spirit illumines the believer. That is, the Spirit brings to the Christian greater cognitive understanding of the biblical text.[3] Theologians also affirm the Spirit's related work of bringing conviction, that is, impressing upon the believer's conscience that the teachings of Scripture are in fact true, applicable, and incumbent upon the reader.

It is also important to note what illumination is not. Grant Osborne offers this helpful caveat:

---

3. In his PhD thesis on illumination, Kevin D. Zuber writes, "The results of illumination are seen as primarily cognitive. From this primary result, illumination may also yield an appreciation of and application of the information cognitively gained. Divine illumination enables one to gain a deeper grasp and comprehension of the content of a divine disclosure. One illumined is actually enabled to 'see,' mentally grasp, more of the content than one who is not illumined. The conceptual insight provided by illumination is like the insight one comes to when a line drawing in which one 'sees' an object is suddenly 'seen as' another object. The onlooker simply experiences a conceptual gestalt that enables more of the content to be seen" ("What Is Illumination? A Study in Evangelical Theology Seeking a Biblically Grounded Definition of the Illuminating Work of the Holy Spirit" [PhD thesis, Trinity Evangelical Divinity School, 1996], abstract).

"The Spirit does not whisper to us special reasons which are not otherwise available; rather, he opens our eyes to acknowledge those reasons which *are* available" (1986:234). In other words, the Spirit makes it possible for the reader to use every faculty to discern the Word and apply it. How does this explain the fact that equally spiritual scholars interpret the same passage quite differently? The Spirit makes it possible to overcome our preunderstanding in order to discern the Word, but he does not guarantee that we will do so. On difficult passages we must use every tool we can muster and still will often read a text the way our experience and theological proclivities dictate. . . . Some passages are so ambiguous that more than one interpretation is possible. We must make our hermeneutical choice but remain open to further leading from the Spirit and challenge from our peers. The Spirit enables us to free our minds to the text but does not whisper to us the correct answer.[4]

I will now offer an analogy to help explain how the Holy Spirit helps Christians in reading the Bible. Let's compare studying the Bible to treasure hunting. Imagine two boats, one with a green-shirted treasure hunter (Christian with the Holy Spirit) and another boat with a brown-shirted treasure hunter (non-Christian without the Holy Spirit). Both adventurers stare through the same murky waters. Both see something shimmering at the bottom of the sea. The green-shirted adventurer says, "I see something shiny, and it looks like gold to me. I am going to dive." The brown-shirted adventurer says, "I only see light reflecting on the sand at the bottom of the ocean. I am not going to dive." All other things being equal, the believer is enabled to weigh the evidence before him more accurately and, consequently, experiences the inner compulsion to act that comes along with recognizing the true state of things. This is not to say, however, that believers always see things rightly because of the Spirit's illuminating work. Many other factors affect interpretation, such as the believer's innate intelligence, skills, predispositions, and, not least, his intimacy with and obedience to God.

---

4. Grant R. Osborne, *The Hermeneutical Spiral: A Comprehensive Introduction to Biblical Interpretation*, rev. ed. (Downers Grove, IL: InterVarsity Press, 2006), 436–37. Osborne's quotation is from John Frame, "The Spirit in the Scriptures," in *Hermeneutics, Authority and Canon*, ed. D. A. Carson and John D. Woodbridge (Grand Rapids: Zondervan, 1986), 234.

Biblically speaking, cognition (mental understanding) and volition (choices of the human will) are two sides of the same coin. The biblical authors do not envision a situation in which someone can affirm the correct meaning of the Bible and at the same time refuse to obey it. Analogously, we cannot imagine a normal person sitting in a smoke-filled room, stating, "I affirm cognitively that the fire alarm is going off, but volitionally I am neither capable nor desirous of acting on this fact."

The human mind and will are conjoined in sinful interdependence. The human heart is prone to self-deception, distortion, wickedness, deceit, and self-justification (Jer. 17:9). The person who will not submit to God inevitably distorts the Bible's teaching and/ or his perception of reality to rationalize his ungodly behavior. As the writer of Proverbs warns, "The sluggard says, 'There is a lion outside!' or, 'I will be murdered in the streets!'" (Prov. 22:13). Note, the sluggard does not say, "I am lazy, so I don't want to go out and work."[5] The sinful human heart manufactures evidence to justify its distorted perspective. Moreover, when we reject the truth, God sends greater blindness and the removal of his gracious divine restraint as punishment. As Paul explains to the Christians in Rome, "Since some did not think it worthwhile to retain the knowledge of God, he gave them over to a depraved mind, to do what ought not to be done" (Rom. 1:28). In this verse the interdependence between darkened thinking and wicked deeds is made clear. Similarly, in 2 Thessalonians 2:10–12, Paul affirms, "Nonbelievers perish because they refused to love the truth and so be saved. For this reason God sends them a powerful delusion so that they will believe the lie and so that all will be condemned who have not believed the truth but have delighted in wickedness." The punishment for embracing the darkness of sin is a further darkened mind and the wicked life that flows from such inner darkness.

A few conservative Christian scholars have attempted to deny or redefine the illuminating work of the Spirit, claiming the Bible teaches only that the Spirit affects the will, bringing conviction, but does not aid in cognition.[6] Unfortunately, this newly proposed view does not

---

5. See John Piper's helpful exposition of Proverbs 22:13 in his "Taste and See" article, www.desiringgod.org (September 16, 1998).
6. E.g., Daniel P. Fuller, "The Holy Spirit's Role in Biblical Interpretation," in *Scripture, Tradition, and Interpretation*, ed. W. Ward Gasque and William

take seriously the noetic effects of the fall (that is, how sin distorts the human thought processes) or biblical indications that the Spirit will counteract the sinful inclinations of our minds. As noted above, the Spirit does *not* whisper some secret meaning inaccessible to others,[7] but the Spirit does enable us to perceive facts and judge the plausibility of arguments with greater clarity. If we believe that God will give a doctor wisdom in diagnosing a disease (as Christians' prayers would indicate), or a college student increased mental concentration on a calculus test, why would God not also give assistance to our weak minds in studying the Bible? Indeed, as the Bible says that God gives teachers to the church (Eph. 4:11–16), would that not indicate, at the least, that *some* in the church are illumined by the Holy Spirit?

The fact that nonbelievers can understand portions of the Scripture does not deny the illuminating work of the Spirit but points to God's common grace in giving all humans (regenerate and nonregenerate) rational minds. (Similarly, nonbelievers made in the image of God can act lovingly without having come to truly love God or love others.) Moreover, nonbelievers' intermittent correct readings of the Bible testify to the clarity of God's revelation. Even hearts in willful rebellion against God sometimes cannot miss his point. Finally, the fact that sincere, godly, Jesus-loving, Bible-believing scholars continue to disagree about the interpretation of some texts does not deny the illuminating work of the Spirit. The amount of disagreement among Bible-believing scholars is easily overstated, and in those cases where disagreement continues (on the proper meaning of baptism, for example), the ongoing disagreement only demonstrates the biases that remain among God's people in spite of his Spirit's work. The Scriptures themselves indicate that, until Jesus returns, believers will continue to disagree on secondary matters. Paul writes:

Sanford LaSor (Grand Rapids: Eerdmans, 1978), 189–98; Robert H. Stein, *A Basic Guide to Interpreting the Bible: Playing by the Rules,* 2nd ed. (Grand Rapids: Baker, 2011), 60–66.

7. We can easily dismiss the assertion of Alan F. Johnson, who writes, "Since the Holy Spirit, not the human authors, is the ultimate Author of Scripture, meanings of the text unknown and unintended by the human authors are possible to discover through the continuing direct revelatory work of the Holy Spirit to believers, both in their reading of the Bible and apart from Scripture" (foreword to *Beyond the Obvious: Discover the Deeper Meaning of Scripture,* by James DeYoung and Sarah Hurty [Gresham, OR: Vision House, 1995], 13).

One man considers one day more sacred than another; another man considers every day alike. *Each one should be fully convinced in his own mind.* He who regards one day as special, does so to the Lord. He who eats meat, eats to the Lord, for he gives thanks to God; and he who abstains, does so to the Lord and gives thanks to God. For none of us lives to himself alone and none of us dies to himself alone. If we live, we live to the Lord; and if we die, we die to the Lord. So, whether we live or die, we belong to the Lord. (Rom. 14:5–8, my emphasis)

Only God knows how many of our theological viewpoints are truly motivated by self-interest, bias, and denominational or ecclesiastical chauvinism rather than a genuine Spirit-led conviction. We must pray with the psalmist,

Who can discern his errors? Forgive my hidden faults. Keep your servant also from willful sins; may they not rule over me. Then will I be blameless, innocent of great transgression. May the words of my mouth and the meditation of my heart be pleasing in your sight, O Lord, my Rock and my Redeemer. (Ps. 19:12–14)

Biblical Texts Supporting Illumination

Listed below is a sampling of biblical texts that support the doctrine of illumination.

- *Psalm 119:17–20: [The psalmist, praying to God] "Do good to your servant, and I will live; I will obey your word. Open my eyes that I may see wonderful things in your law. I am a stranger on earth; do not hide your commands from me. My soul is consumed with longing for your laws at all times."* The authors of the psalms pray repeatedly for divine assistance in understanding and applying God's Word (see, for example, the many petitions in Ps. 119).

- *Matthew 13:11–16: "[Jesus] replied, 'The knowledge of the secrets of the kingdom of heaven has been given to you [i.e., the disciples], but not to them [i.e., nonbelieving outsiders]. Whoever has will be given more, and he will have an abundance. Whoever does not have, even what he has will be taken from him. This is why I speak to them in parables: "Though seeing, they do not see;*

*though hearing, they do not hear or understand." In them is ful-
filled the prophecy of Isaiah: "You will be ever hearing but never
understanding; you will be ever seeing but never perceiving. For
this people's heart has become calloused; they hardly hear with
their ears, and they have closed their eyes. Otherwise they might
see with their eyes, hear with their ears, understand with their
hearts and turn, and I would heal them." But blessed are your
eyes because they see, and your ears because they hear.'"* In this
passage, Jesus differentiates his followers from those outside.
His followers are able to truly see, hear, and understand Jesus'
teaching because it has been "given" to them by God (i.e., they
have received divine assistance).

- *1 Corinthians 2:14: "The man without the Spirit does not accept
  the things that come from the Spirit of God, for they are foolishness to him, and he cannot understand them, because they
  are spiritually discerned."* In this passage, "the things that come
  from the Spirit of God" are the verbal and written proclama-
  tions of the gospel from Paul. The volitional rejection of God's
  message by nonbelievers is integrally related to their sinfully
  distorted cognition.

- *2 Corinthians 3:13–16: "We are not like Moses, who would put
  a veil over his face to keep the Israelites from gazing at it while
  the radiance was fading away. But their minds were made dull,
  for to this day the same veil remains when the old covenant is
  read. It has not been removed, because only in Christ is it taken
  away. Even to this day when Moses is read, a veil covers their
  hearts. But whenever anyone turns to the Lord, the veil is taken
  away."* Here Paul speaks of nonbelieving Jews as having dull
  minds and veiled hearts—metaphorical language to describe
  the blindness and hardness they demonstrate in failing to acknowledge how the Scriptures point to Messiah Jesus (see also
  Rom. 11:7–8).

- *Luke 24:44–45: "He said to them, 'This is what I told you while
  I was still with you: Everything must be fulfilled that is written
  about me in the Law of Moses, the Prophets and the Psalms.' Then
  he opened their minds so they could understand the Scriptures."
  John 20:22: "And with that he breathed on them and said,*

'Receive the Holy Spirit.'" These parallel passages describe the same resurrection appearance of Jesus from different vantage points. It is striking that what Luke describes as the opening of the disciples' minds to understand the Scriptures, John describes as the reception of the Holy Spirit. Only by the Spirit's aid can we rightly perceive Christ as the ultimate meaning of the Bible.

Practical Implications of Illumination

If the Bible teaches that the Holy Spirit helps believers in understanding, applying, and obeying Scripture (as argued above), then there are clear implications for the way we should approach the Bible. While showing due diligence in reading, studying, researching, and thinking, the Christian ultimately must bow before the divine author of Scripture to confess his sinfulness and seek supernatural aid. Studying the Bible must begin with prayer and worship.

REFLECTION QUESTIONS

1. Have you ever heard someone appeal to the Holy Spirit to support a meaning of Scripture that seemed to you an illegitimate interpretation? How did you handle the situation?

2. Of the two views about the Spirit's role in biblical interpretation presented above (traditional illumination view versus the Spirit only aids in volition), which do you think is correct? Why? (Or, is there some other view of the Spirit's work you espouse?)

3. If the view on illumination presented above is correct, how should that affect the way you personally study the Bible?

4. If the view on illumination presented above is correct, how should that affect the way you talk about the Bible with others?

5. Pray this prayer slowly and thoughtfully prior to reading your Bible:

A Prayer of Illumination

> Living God,
> help us to hear your holy Word with open hearts
> so that we may truly understand;
> and, understanding,
> that we may believe;
> and, believing,
> that we may follow in all faithfulness and obedience,
> Seeking your honor and glory in all that we do.
> Through Christ, our Lord. Amen.[8]

---

8. Huldrych Zwingli (1484–1531), altered, as collected in *The Worship Sourcebook*, ed. Emily R. Brink and John D. Witvliet (Grand Rapids: Baker; Calvin Institute of Worship; Faith Alive Christian Resources, 2004), 142.

FOR FURTHER STUDY

Ferguson, Sinclair B. *The Holy Spirit.* Contours of Christian Theology. Downers Grove, IL: InterVarsity Press, 1997.

Thompson, Mark D. *A Clear and Present Word: The Clarity of Scripture.* New Studies in Biblical Theology. Vol. 21. Downers Grove, IL: InterVarsity Press, 2006.

CHAPTER 7

The Overarching Message of the Bible

Consisting of sixty-six distinct works written over more than a millennium and a half, the Bible can be an intimidating book. Is there an overarching message to the Bible? How do the seemingly disparate parts fit together? What is the big picture we should keep in mind as we look at smaller portions of Scripture?

The Person and Saving Work of Jesus Christ

Whatever portion of the Bible one is studying, it is important to remember that the person and saving work of Jesus Christ is the ultimate focus of God's revelation. To his contemporaries, Jesus said, "You diligently study the Scriptures because you think that by them you possess eternal life. These are the Scriptures that testify about me" (John 5:39). Likewise, the gospel of Luke tells us that when Jesus spoke with two disciples on the road to Emmaus, "Beginning with Moses and all the Prophets, he explained to them what was said in all the Scriptures concerning himself" (Luke 24:27). The author of Hebrews writes,

> In the past God spoke to our forefathers through the prophets at many times and in various ways, but in these last days he has spoken to us by his Son, whom he appointed heir of all things, and through whom he made the universe. The Son is the radiance of God's glory and the exact representation of his being, sustaining all things by his powerful word. After he had provided purification for sins, he sat down at the right hand of the Majesty in heaven. So he became as much superior to the angels as the name he has inherited is superior to theirs. (Heb. 1:1–4)

From the outset, the Bible establishes that though God created a perfect world, humans destroyed that perfection through their rebellion (Gen. 1–3). Only through the promised Messiah (Christ) would the creation be restored to perfect communion with its Creator (Gen. 3:15). The story line of the Bible reveals the need for Jesus, the promise of Jesus, the anticipation of Jesus, the incarnation/arrival of Jesus, the teachings of Jesus, the crucifixion of Jesus, the resurrection of Jesus, the ascension of Jesus, and the promised return of Jesus. The Bible is a book about Jesus.

With this assumed Christocentric foundation, we will now suggest a few additional organizing categories that can be helpful in seeing the big picture of the Bible's message.

Promise-Fulfillment

In the Sermon on the Mount, Jesus said, "Do not think that I have come to abolish the Law or the Prophets; I have not come to abolish them but to fulfill them" (Matt. 5:17). Thus, in speaking of the Bible, Jesus uses the categories of anticipation/promise (for the Old Testament) and fulfillment (for his life, death, and resurrection). We see a similar framework in Matthew 11:12–13, where Jesus makes clear the preparatory nature of the Old Testament and the inauguration of long-awaited promises through the preaching of the messianic forerunner, John the Baptist. Jesus says, "From the days of John the Baptist until now, the kingdom of heaven has been forcefully advancing, and forceful men lay hold of it. For all the Prophets and the Law prophesied until John."

Again, though the words *promise* and *fulfillment* are not explicitly used in 1 Peter 1:9–12, the passage contains these same ideas. The apostle Peter writes to believers in Rome:

> You are receiving the goal of your faith, the salvation of your souls. Concerning this salvation, the prophets, who spoke of the grace that was to come to you, searched intently and with the greatest care, trying to find out the time and circumstances to which the Spirit of Christ in them was pointing when he predicted the sufferings of Christ and the glories that would follow. It was revealed to them that they were not serving themselves but you, when they spoke of the things that have now been told you by those who have preached the gospel to you by the Holy Spirit sent from heaven. Even angels long to look into these things. (1 Peter 1:9–12)

Thus, in reading the Bible, one can ask this basic question: Am I reading the promise or fulfillment part of Scripture? In what way is Christ anticipated in this text, or in what way is his arrival heralded?

Kingdom Anticipated—Kingdom Inaugurated— Kingdom Consummated

When Jesus began his itinerant teaching ministry, he announced the arrival of the kingdom of God (Mark 1:15).[1] Jesus was not announcing that there was a kingdom but that the expected kingdom was inaugurated in his life and ministry.[2] Throughout the Old Testament, God is repeatedly referred to as king over all of creation, especially over Israel (1 Chron. 29:11; Dan. 4:32; Obad. 21; Pss. 22:27–28; 103:19; 145:11–13). God's divine kingship is mediated to Israel through the prophets, judges, and human kings (1 Sam. 8:4–9; Ps. 2:6–7), but a day is anticipated when God's kingship will be universally acknowledged (Ps. 67). Jesus declares that in him, the inbreaking of God's final, decisive eschatological reign is taking place (Matt. 12:28). Yet, Jesus also speaks of the consummation of God's kingdom in the future, when God's people will rest in the presence of God and God's enemies will be subdued (Matt. 8:11). Sometimes scholars speak of the "already" and "not yet" dimensions of God's kingdom in the New Testament. The kingdom already has arrived in Jesus' life, death, and resurrection, but the kingdom is not yet fully present.[3] While forcefully advancing and amazingly productive, the kingdom is not fully and universally instituted (Matt. 11:12–13; Mark 4:26–32).

Several biblical scholars have offered detailed frameworks based around the kingdom motif in the Bible.[4] Also, an influential children's Bible that tries to teach the big picture of the Bible using "kingdom" as a significant organizing principle was recently published. Fittingly, this children's Bible is titled *The Big Picture Story Bible*. While I see

---

1. The terms "kingdom of heaven," "kingdom of God," and "kingdom," though having slightly different nuances, are used interchangeably in the New Testament.
2. Leonhard Goppelt, *Theology of the New Testament*, ed. Jürgen Roloff, trans. John E. Alsup (Grand Rapids: Eerdmans, 1981), 1:45.
3. George E. Ladd, *A Theology of the New Testament*, ed. Donald A. Hagner, rev. ed. (Grand Rapids: Eerdmans, 1974), 61–67; and idem, *Jesus and the Kingdom: The Eschatology of Biblical Realism* (New York: Harper & Row, 1964).
4. E.g., Graeme Goldsworthy, *Gospel and Kingdom: A Christian Interpretation of the Old Testament*, 2nd ed. (Carlisle, UK: Paternoster, 1994).

FIGURE 1: THE KINGDOM OF GOD IN THE BIBLE	
KINGDOM STAGES	**BIBLICAL/HISTORICAL PERIOD**
The Pattern of the Kingdom	Genesis 1–2
The Perished Kingdom	Genesis 3
The Promised Kingdom	Genesis 12:1–3
The Partial Kingdom	Genesis 12—2 Chronicles (Patriarchs, Exodus, Law, Conquest, Monarchy)
The Prophesied Kingdom	Ezra—Malachi
The Present Kingdom	The Gospels (the birth, life, death and resurrection of Christ)
The Proclaimed Kingdom	Acts—Revelation
The Perfected Kingdom	Inaugurated at Jesus' Second Coming

Source: Vaughan Roberts, *God's Big Picture: Tracing the Storyline of the Bible* (Downers Grove, IL: InterVarsity Press, 2002), 157. Used by permission.

much that is good in approaching the Bible through the grid of kingdom (see figure 1), I offer three caveats. (1) There is a danger of losing the Christ-centered nature of Scripture by focusing on the kingdom. Ultimately, Christ is the king and the kingdom is present in him. "The kingdom advances here on earth *where faith and obedience to Christ are found*."[5] (2) Some attempts to explain portions of Scripture with kingdom language, while quite clever, go beyond any explicit references to kingdom in the actual biblical text. (3) In an attempt to systematize the Bible under the theme of kingdom, some

5. Mark Seifrid, "Introduction to the New Testament: Historical Background and Gospels, Course Number NT 22200" (unpublished notes, Southern Baptist Theological Seminary, fall 1998), 54.

poignant details of the text can be overlooked. For example, after I read the account of the conquering of Jericho to my four-year-old daughter from *The Big Picture Story Bible*, her response was, "Where is the lady? Why did they leave out the lady?" The author of the children's Bible had left Rahab and her heroic faith out of the story.

Old Covenant—New Covenant

Another way of thinking about the Bible as a whole is to employ the idea of covenant. A covenant establishes the basis of a relationship and the expectations of the parties involved, as well as consequences for not meeting those expectations. Biblically, the relationship between God and human beings is founded upon a covenant (Gen. 17:1–14; Exod. 2:23–25; 20:1–24:18; Jer. 31:31–34; Luke 22:20; 1 Cor. 11:25). As humans are in active rebellion against God and undeserving of a relationship with him, covenants between God and humans are always based on God's undeserved kindness and self-disclosure.

The underlying covenantal basis of biblical revelation is made clear in Jeremiah 31:31–34. The text reads:

> "Behold, days are coming," declares the LORD, "when I will make a new covenant with the house of Israel and with the house of Judah, not like the covenant which I made with their fathers in the day I took them by the hand to bring them out of the land of Egypt, My covenant which they broke, although I was a husband to them," declares the LORD. "But this is the covenant which I will make with the house of Israel after those days," declares the LORD, "I will put My law within them and on their heart I will write it; and I will be their God, and they shall be My people. They will not teach again, each man his neighbor and each man his brother, saying, 'Know the LORD,' for they will all know Me, from the least of them to the greatest of them," declares the LORD, "for I will forgive their iniquity, and their sin I will remember no more." (NASB)

God describes the relationship between himself and Israel as based on a covenant made at Sinai (cf. Exod. 20–24). But according to the text above, the covenant was broken by Israel's repeated sin. A coming new covenant is promised that will be radically different from the old. The new covenant results in a forgiven people who know the Lord and have his requirements written on their hearts.

Jesus declared that his atoning death instituted this promised new covenant (Luke 22:20; Heb. 8:6–13; 12:24).

Covenantal theology, a common Reformed approach to the Scriptures, attempts to view all post-fall relationship between God and his people under the canopy of a covenant of grace. Nevertheless, the old covenant-new covenant distinction present in Scripture would lead us to eschew the term "covenant of grace" in favor of more explicit biblical categories.

Conceptually parallel to the distinction between old and new covenants, the apostle John writes, "For the law was given through Moses; grace and truth came through Jesus Christ" (John 1:17). One should not understand the old covenant stipulations as intending to save or transform (and thus not subsumed under a covenant of grace) but primarily as intending to prophesy and prepare for the necessity of the new covenant instituted by Messiah Jesus. The theological system that attempts to systematize the Bible through the lens of old and new covenant, especially focusing on the "newness" brought in Jesus, is called "new covenant theology."[6]

Noting the biblical basis for covenantal distinctions (e.g., Jer. 31:31–34), a key question to ask in reading the Scriptures is whether the passage reflects the old or new covenant. During the administration of the old covenant, there were many institutions and laws that were preparatory in nature. As the author of Hebrews says, "The law is only a shadow of the good things that are coming—not the realities themselves. For this reason it can never, by the same sacrifices repeated endlessly year after year, make perfect those who draw near to worship" (Heb. 10:1). Under the old covenant, God's people discovered experientially that they were unable to keep his laws and in need of a more radical solution—a spiritual rebirth and a righteousness that comes from outside, a righteousness from God himself (John 1:9–13; Rom. 3:19–26).

Law-Gospel

Similar to the old and new covenant distinctions, one also can view the Bible through the grid of law and gospel. Paul certainly seems to make a distinction between the law and gospel in his writings. In Galatians 3:23–25, the apostle writes:

---

6. See Tom Wells and Fred Zaspel, *New Covenant Theology: Description, Definition, Defense* (Frederick, MD: New Covenant Media, 2002).

Before the way of faith in Christ was available to us, we were placed under guard by the law. We were kept in protective custody, so to speak, until the way of faith was revealed. Let me put it another way. The law was our guardian until Christ came; it protected us until we could be made right with God through faith. And now that the way of faith has come, we no longer need the law as our guardian. (NLT)

It would seem, then, that a *sine qua non* (an essential prerequisite) of biblical theology is the distinction between the preparatory law and the promised gospel.

One of the most outspoken advocates of the law-gospel distinction was the reformer Martin Luther (1483–1546). With reference to his conversion, Luther declared,

I learned to distinguish between the righteousness of the law and the righteousness of the gospel. I lacked nothing before this except that I made no distinction between the law and the gospel. I regarded both as the same thing and held that there was no difference between Christ and Moses except the times in which they lived and their degrees of perfection. But when I discovered the proper distinction—namely, that the law is one thing and the gospel is another—I made myself free.[7]

The difference between law and gospel is explained briefly in these two sentences:

The law says, "Do this, and you will live."

The gospel says, "It is done. Now, live."[8]

Any portion of Scripture can be divided into "demand" (law) or "grace-gift" (gospel). The demands of Scripture are incumbent upon

---

7. Martin Luther, *Table Talk*, vol. 54, in *Luther's Works*, ed. J. Pelikan, H. Oswald, and H. Lehmann (Philadelphia: Fortress, 1967), 442.

8. Luther writes, "I must hearken to the Gospel, which teacheth me, not what I ought to do (for that is the proper office of the Law), but what Jesus Christ the Son of God hath done for me: to wit, that he suffered and died to deliver me from sin and death" (Martin Luther, *A Commentary on St. Paul's Epistle to the Galatians* [London: James Clarke, 1953], 101).

us, but because of our sin-stained hearts, minds, and wills, even our most righteous acts are like filthy rags in God's sight (Isa. 64:6). As Paul writes, "For no one can ever be made right with God by doing what the law commands. The law simply shows us how sinful we are" (Rom. 3:20 NLT). God's demands reveal our incurable moral sickness and drive us to his gracious promises in the gospel. We then can cling to Jesus' words in John 6:37: "All that the Father gives me will come to me, and whoever comes to me I will never drive away." Similarly, Paul writes:

> But now God has shown us a way to be made right with him without keeping the requirements of the law, as was promised in the writings of Moses and the prophets long ago. We are made right with God by placing our faith in Jesus Christ. And this is true for everyone who believes, no matter who we are. For everyone has sinned; we all fall short of God's glorious standard. Yet God, with undeserved kindness, declares that we are righteous. He did this through Christ Jesus when he freed us from the penalty for our sins. (Rom. 3:21–24 NLT)

All biblical Christians would agree that at least one of the functions of the Old Testament laws was to point out human moral bankruptcy and lead the sinner to Christ (Gal. 3:23–25). But what of the moral demands in the New Testament? While it is clear that the New Testament writers expected Jesus' followers to have truly changed behavior because of the indwelling Spirit (1 Cor. 6:9–11; 1 John 2:4), it is also true that Jesus' followers remain people who "stumble in many ways" (James 3:2). A Christian who says that he is without sin is a liar (1 John 1:8–10). Undoubtedly, in the new covenant period, there is new empowerment to enable the Lord's people to reflect his character. Yet we are imperfectly transformed, which makes us rely on Christ's righteousness and long for his return and the promised transformation of our bodies (1 John 3:2). Only in the final state, as we stand eternally changed in Jesus' presence, will we be completely free from sin.

Salvation History

"Salvation history" is the usual English translation of the German term *Heilsgeschichte* (literally, in German, "holy history"), a term popularized by Oscar Cullmann (1902–1999). *Salvation history* is an expression used to summarize all of biblical revelation, culminating in the central saving event of Christ's life, death, and resurrection. That is, the Bible is a story of God intervening in history to save a people for himself. While this assertion is obviously true, the categorization of the entire Bible as "salvation history" (or "redemptive history") is so broad that it is questionable how helpful it is in explaining how the pieces of the Bible fit together. Still, it can be beneficial to ask, "In what ways does this passage reveal God's progressive, saving revelation of himself to wayward humans?" Or, "Where does this passage fit into God's saving plan—is it anticipatory, climactic, or looking backward to God's culminating intervention in Christ" (see Heb. 1:1–3)?

Dispensationalism

While not advocated in this book, dispensationalism is another method for explaining the unity of the Bible. Dispensationalism is an approach to the Bible that is characterized by a sharp distinction between God's plans for ethnic Israel and God's plan for the church. Also, dispensationalists have an admitted bias toward reading the Bible, especially prophecies, as literal whenever possible. Figurative or symbolic approaches to Old Testament prophecy, especially those that concern Israel, are viewed with great suspicion.[9]

There is great diversity among dispensationalists, but the traditional dispensationalism—made popular by notes in the Scofield Reference Bible—divides biblical history into seven God-human arrangements, or dispensations. Most dispensations consist of a divine self-disclosure, human failure, and resulting judgment. The seven dispensations classically taught are:

1. Dispensation of Innocence (Gen. 1:3–3:6, Creation to the Fall).

2. Dispensation of Conscience (Gen. 3:7–8:14, The Fall to the Flood).

3. Dispensation of Civil Government (Gen. 8:15–11:9, Rainbow Covenant with Noah to the Tower of Babel).

---

9. Charles C. Ryrie, a prominent dispensationalist scholar, writes, "The essence of dispensationalism is (1) the recognition of a consistent distinction between Israel and the church, (2) a consistent and regular use of a literal principle of interpretation, and (3) a basic and primary conception of the purpose of God as His own glory rather than the salvation of mankind" (*Dispensationalism*, rev. ed. [Chicago: Moody Press, 1995], 45).

4. Dispensation of Patriarchal Rule (Gen 11:10–Exod. 18:27, Abraham to the Exodus).

5. Dispensation of Mosaic Law (Exod. 19:1–Acts 1:26, Moses to the death of Christ).

6. Dispensation of Grace (Acts 2:1–Rev. 19:21, Pentecost to the second coming of Christ. The tribulation period is the judgment of persons who rejected Christ in this dispensation.).

7. Dispensation of the Millennium (Rev. 20:1–15, Post-Advent thousand-year reign of Christ, ending in the Great White Throne judgment).[10]

Dispensationalists are also well known for teaching the "secret rapture" of the church, a view first promulgated in the 1830s by the father of dispensationalism, J. N. Darby. Many members of evangelical churches in America have unwittingly adopted dispensationalist views—especially on end-times issues. This influence has come through books such as *The Late Great Planet Earth* and the *Left Behind* books and movies.

Recognizing weaknesses in traditional dispensationalism, a new and influential movement called progressive dispensationalism has emerged within evangelicalism. Like traditional dispensationalists, progressives maintain a distinction between Israel and the church and the expectation of a literal millennial kingdom. Yet, there are significant differences. Progressive dispensationalist scholars generally contend for fewer dispensations or salvation-historical periods—allowing the explicit covenants of Scripture (Abrahamic, Davidic, New) to have greater hermeneutical influence. Sometimes progressives are charged with having created a mediating position between traditional dispensationalism and covenant theology. With the disapproval of most traditional dispensationalists, progressives are also readier to acknowledge nonliteral fulfillments of some Old Testament prophecies in the New Testament, as well as the emerging presence of Jesus' Davidic reign in the current age.[11]

10. This list is derived from Ryrie, *Dispensationalism*, 51–57.
11. See Craig A. Blaising and Darrell L. Bock, *Progressive Dispensationalism* (Wheaton, IL: BridgePoint, 1993).

REFLECTION QUESTIONS

1. What is the overarching message of the Bible?

2. While reading through the above sections, did you recognize a theological system or framework that has been presented to you in the past?

3. Did any of the organizing structures presented above help you see more clearly the big picture of the Bible?

4. Which of the interpretive grids seems most faithful to the explicit language of Scripture?

5. Read aloud this hymn by Isaac Watts ("The Law Commands and Makes Us Know"). Ask yourself, "Have I personally experienced the freedom of the gospel spoken of here?"

> The Law commands and makes us know
> What duties to our God we owe;
> But 'tis the Gospel must reveal
> Where lies our strength to do His will.
> The Law discovers guilt and sin,
> And shows how vile our hearts have been;
> Only the Gospel can express
> Forgiving love and cleansing grace.
> What curses doth the Law denounce
> Against the man that fails but once!
> But in the Gospel Christ appears
> Pard'ning the guilt of num'rous years.
> My soul, no more attempt to draw
> Thy life and comfort from the Law;
> Fly to the hope the Gospel gives;
> The man that trusts the promise lives.

FOR FURTHER STUDY

Goldsworthy, Graeme. *According to Plan: The Unfolding Revelation of God in the Bible*. Downers Grove, IL: InterVarsity Press, 1991.
_____. *Gospel and Kingdom: A Christian Interpretation of the Old Testament*. 2nd ed. Carlisle, UK: Paternoster, 1994.
_____. *Gospel-Centered Hermeneutics: Foundations and Principles of Evangelical Biblical Interpretation*. Downers Grove, IL: InterVarsity Press, 2006.
Helm, David. *The Big Picture Story Bible*. Illustrated by Gail Schoonmaker. Wheaton, IL: Crossway, 2004. (A children's Bible but beneficial for adults to see the Christological theme of Scripture.)
Lloyd-Jones, Sally. *The Jesus Storybook Bible*. Illustrated by Jago. Grand Rapids: ZonderKidz, 2007. (Another children's Bible but beneficial for adults to see the Christological theme of Scripture.)
Roberts, Vaughan. *God's Big Picture: Tracing the Storyline of the Bible*. Downers Grove, IL: InterVarsity Press, 2002.
Seifrid, Mark A. "Rightly Dividing the Word of Truth: An Introduction to the Distinction Between Law and Gospel." *Southern Baptist Journal of Theology* 10, no. 2 (2006): 56–68.

Select Bibliography

Archer, Gleason. *A Survey of Old Testament Introduction.* Rev. ed. Chicago: Moody Press, 1994.

Beale, G. K. *The Erosion of Inerrancy in Evangelicalism: Responding to New Challenges to Biblical Authority.* Wheaton, IL: Crossway, 2008.

Bruce, F. F. *The New Testament Documents: Are They Reliable?* 6th ed. Downers Grove, IL: InterVarsity Press; Grand Rapids: Eerdmans, 1981.

Carson, D. A. *For the Love of God: A Daily Companion for Discovering the Riches of God's Word.* Vols. 1 and 2. Wheaton, IL: Crossway, 1998, 1999.

_____. *New Testament Commentary Survey.* 6th ed. Grand Rapids: Baker, 2007.

Carson, D. A., and Douglas J. Moo. *An Introduction to the New Testament.* 2nd ed. Grand Rapids: Zondervan, 2005.

ESV Study Bible. Wheaton, IL: Crossway, 2008.

Evans, Craig A. *Fabricating Jesus: How Modern Scholars Distort the Gospels.* Downers Grove, IL: InterVarsity Press, 2008.

Fee, Gordon D., and Mark L. Strauss. *How to Choose a Translation for All Its Worth.* Grand Rapids: Zondervan, 2007.

Glynn, John. *Commentary and Reference Survey: A Comprehensive Guide to Biblical and Theological Resources.* 10th ed. Grand Rapids: Kregel, 2007.

Grudem, Wayne. *Systematic Theology: An Introduction to Biblical Doctrine.* Grand Rapids: Zondervan; Leicester: Inter-Varsity Press, 1994.

Longman, Tremper. *Old Testament Commentary Survey.* 4th ed. Grand Rapids: Baker, 2007.

Plummer, Robert L. *40 Questions About Interpreting the Bible.* Grand Rapids: Kregel, 2010.

Stein, Robert H. *A Basic Guide to Interpreting the Bible: Playing by the Rules, 2nd ed.* Grand Rapids: Baker, 2011.

Wegner, Paul D. *The Journey from Texts to Translations: The Origin and Development of the Bible.* Grand Rapids: Baker, 1999.

Zondervan NIV Study Bible, Rev. ed. Edited by Kenneth L. Barker, et al. Grand Rapids: Zondervan, 2008.